D0151124

For we are not children of the bond-woman, but of the free.

E pur se muove.

OUTLINES

OF A

CRITICAL THEORY OF ETHICS

BY

JOHN DEWEY

Professor of Philosophy in the University of Michigan

GREENWOOD PRESS, PUBLISHERS
NEW YORK

Originally published in 1891 and reprinted in 1957 by Hillary House, Inc.

Reprinted in 1969 by Greenwood Press, Inc.,
51 Riverside Avenue, Westport, CT 06880

Library of Congress catalog card number 71-92299
ISBN 0-8371-2707-6

Printed in the United States of America

10 9 8 7 6 5 4 3 2

CONTENTS.

PART III.—THE MORAL LIFE OF THE INDIVIDUAL.

PREFACE.

ALTHOUGH the following pages have taken shape in connection with class-room work, they are intended as an independent contribution to ethical science. It is commonly demanded of such a work that its readers shall have some prefatory hint of its sources and deviations. In accordance with this custom, I may state that for the backbone of the theory here presented—the conception of the will as the expression of ideas, and of social ideas; the notion of an objective ethical world realized in institutions which afford moral ideals, theatre and impetus to the individual; the notion of the moral life as growth in freedom, as the individual finds and conforms to the law of his social placing—for this backbone I am especially indebted to Green's 'Prolegomena to Ethics', to Mr. Bradley's 'Ethical Studies', to Professor Caird's 'Social Philosophy of Comte' and 'Critical Philosophy of Kant' (to this latter book in particular my indebtedness is fundamental), and to Alexander's 'Moral Order and Progress'. Although I have not been able to adopt the stand-point or the method of Mr. Spencer, or of Mr. Leslie Stephen my obligation to the 'Data of Ethics' and to the 'Science of Ethics' (especially to the latter) is large.

As to the specific forms which give a flesh and blood of its own to this backbone, I may call attention to the idea of desire as the ideal activity in contrast with actual possession; to the analysis of individuality into function including capacity and environment; to the treatment of the social bearings of science and art (a point concerning which I am indebted to my friend, Mr. Franklin Ford); to the statement of an ethical postulate; to the accounts of obligation, of moral rules, and of moral badness.

While the book is an analysis, in outline, of the main elements of the theory of ethics rather than a discussion of all possible detailed questions, it will not be found the less fitted, I hope, to give a student an idea of the main methods and problems of contemporary ethics. Other teachers, indeed, may agree that a general outline is better than a blanket-mortgage spread over and forestalling all the activity of the student's mind.

I have not been unmindful of the advisability of avoiding in presentation both undue polemic, and undue dogmatism without sufficient reference to the statements of others. I hope the method hit upon, of comparing opposite one-sided views with the aim of discovering a theory apparently more adequate, will help keep the balance. I have quoted freely from the chief modern authorities, hoping that the tastes here given will tempt the reader to the banquet waiting in the authors themselves. The occasional references introduced are not bibliographical, nor intended as exhaustive statements of authorities consulted; they are meant as aids to an intelligent reading on the part of the general student. For this reason they are confined mainly to modern English writings.

INTRODUCTION.

I.

Definition of Ethics. The term ethics is derived from a Greek word meaning manners, customs, habits, just as the term morals is derived from a Latin word with a similar meaning. This suggests the character of the science as an account of human action. Anthropology, ethnology, psychology, are also, in their way, accounts of human action. But these latter branches of knowledge simply *describe*, while the business of ethics is to *judge.*

This does not mean that it belongs to ethics to prescribe what man ought to do; but that its business is to detect the element of obligation in conduct, to examine conduct to see what gives it its *worth.* Anthropology, etc., do not take into account the *whole* of action, but simply some of its aspects—either external or internal. Ethics deals with conduct in its entirety, with reference, that is, to what makes it conduct, its *end*, its real meaning. Ethics is the science of conduct, understanding by conduct man's activity in its whole reach.

Three of the branches of philosophy may be called *normative*, implying that they deal with some *norm*, *standard* or *end*, estimating the value of their respective subject-matters as tested by this end These are Logic, dealing with the end Truth, and the value of intellectual processes with respect to it; Æsthetics, dealing with Beauty and the value of emotional conditions as referred to it; and Ethics, as defined above. But this norm in no case comes from outside the subject-matter; it is the subject-matter considered in its totality.

II.

Meaning of Moral. In its widest sense, the term moral or ethical means nothing more than relating to conduct; having to do with practice, when we look at conduct or practice from the point of view not of its occurrence, but of its value. Action is something which takes place, and as such it may be described like any objective fact. But action has also relation to an end, and so considered it is *moral.* The first step in ethics is to fix firmly in mind the idea that the term moral does not mean any special or peculiar kind of conduct, but simply means practice and action, conduct viewed not partially, but in connection with the end which it realizes.

It should be noted that the term moral has a wider and a narrower sense. In the wider sense it means action in the moral sphere, as opposed to *non*-moral, and thus includes both good and bad conduct. In the narrower sense it means moral, as opposed to *im*-moral. See Bradley, Ethical Studies, p. 53, note, for a further meaning.

III.

Meaning of Conduct. Ethics then has to do with conduct or action viewed completely, or in relation to its end. But what is conduct? It must be distinguished from action in general; for any process of change, the working of a pump, the growth of a plant, the barking of a dog, may be called action. Conduct implies more than something taking place; it implies purpose, motive, intention; that the agent knows what he is about, that he has something which he is aiming at. All action accomplishes something or brings about results, but conduct has the result *in view.* It occurs for the sake of producing this result. Conduct does not simply, like action in general, have a cause, but also a reason, and the reason is present to the mind of the agent. There can be conduct only when there is a being who can propose to himself, as an end to be reached by himself, something which he regards as worth while. Such a being is a moral agent, and his action, when conscious, is conduct.

IV.

Division of Ethics. The main ethical problem is just this: What is the conduct that really deserves the name of conduct, the conduct of which all other kinds of action can be only a perverted or deflected form? Or, since it is the end which gives action its moral value, what is the true end, *summum bonum* of man? Knowing this, we have a standard by which we judge particular acts. Those which embody this end are *right*, others wrong. The question of the rightness of conduct is simply a special form of the question concerning the nature of the end or good. But the end bears another relation to specific acts. They are not only marked off by it as right or wrong, but they have to fulfill it. The end or good decides what should be or *ought* to be. Any act necessary to fulfill the end is a *duty*. Our second inquiry will be as to the nature of obligation or duty. Then we have to discuss the nature of a being who is capable of action, of manifesting and realizing the end; capable of right (or wrong) of obligatory and good action. This will lead us to discuss the question of *Freedom, or Moral Capacity and its Realization.* The discussion of these three abstract questions will constitute Part I of our theory; Part II will take up the various forms and institutions in which the good is objectively realized, the family, state, etc.; while Part III will be devoted to an account of the moral experience of the individual.

V.

The Motive in Conduct. Before taking up the first problem presented, the nature of the good or the end of conduct, it is necessary to analyze somewhat further the various sides and factors of conduct in order to see where the distinctly ethical element is to be found. The elements particularly deserving consideration are (1) the Motive; (2) the Feelings or Sentiments; (3) Consequences of the Act; (4) Character of Agent. We shall begin with

1. *The Motive.* The motive of the act is the end aimed at by the agent in performing the act. Thus the motive of Julius Cæsar in crossing the Rubicon was the whole series of results which he intended to reach by that act of his. The motive of a person in coming to college is to gain knowledge, to prepare himself for a certain profession. The motive is thus identical with the ideal element of the action, the purpose in view.

2. *The Feelings or Disposition.* Some writers speak of the feelings under which the agent acts as his motive. Thus we may suppose Julius Cæsar 'moved' by the feelings of ambition, of revenge, etc., in crossing the Rubicon. The student may be 'moved' by curiosity, by vainglory, by emulation, by conscience, in coming to college. It is better, however, to regard the motive as the reason for which the act is performed, and to use the term moving or impelling cause for the feelings in their relation to action. Thus we may imagine a parent asking a child why he struck a playmate, meaning

what was the motive of the action. If the child should reply that he struck his playmate because he was angry, this answer would give the moving cause or impelling force of the action, but not its motive. The motive would be the idea of punishing this playmate, of getting even with him, of taking something away from him. The motive is the end which he desired to reach by striking and on account of which he struck. This is implied by the fact that the parent would ask, "What *made* you *angry?*"

VI.

Moral Bearing of These Distinctions. It is the feelings which supply the impelling force to action. They may be termed, collectively, the *natural disposition.* The natural disposition in itself has no *moral* value. This has been well illustrated by Bentham.

Principles of Morals and Legislation, pp. 49–55. Bentham here uses the term 'motive' to designate what we have called the moving cause.

We may select of the many examples which he gives that of curiosity. We may imagine a boy spinning a top, reading a useful book and letting a wild ox loose in a road. Now curiosity may be the 'motive' of each of these acts, yet the first act would generally be called morally indifferent, the second good, the third abominable.

What we mean by the 'natural' feelings, then, is the feelings considered in abstraction from activity. Benevolence, as a *mere* feeling, has no higher moral value than malevolence. But if it is directed upon action it gets a value at once; let the end, the act, be right, and benevolence becomes a name for a *moral* disposition—a tendency to *act* in the due way. Nothing is more important than to distinguish between mere sentiments, and feeling as an element in conduct.

VII.

Relation of Consequences and Conduct.

Do the consequences of an act have anything to do with its morality? We may say no, pointing to the fact that a man who does his best we call good, although the consequences of his act may be far from good. We say his purpose in acting was right, and using as he did all the knowledge that he had, he is not to be blamed for its bad consequences. On the other hand, it is evident that we do take into account consequences in estimating the moral value of an act. Suppose, to use one of Bentham's examples, a person were about to shoot an animal but foresaw that in doing so there was a strong probability that he would also wound some bystander. If he shot and the spectator were wounded, should we not hold the agent morally responsible? Are there not multitudes of intended acts of which we say that we cannot tell whether they are good or bad until we know how they are likely to turn out?

The solution of the difficulty is in recognizing the ambiguity of the term 'consequences'. It may mean the whole outcome of the act. When I speak, I set in motion the air, and its vibrations have, in turn, long chains of effects. Whatever I do must have an endless succession of 'consequences' of which I can know but very little; just so far as, in any act, I am ignorant of the conditions under which it is performed, so far I am ignorant of its consequences. *Such* consequences are wholly irrelevant morally. They have no more to do with the morality of the act than has the fact that the earth is revolving while the act is taking place.

But we may mean by consequences the *foreseen* consequences of an act. Just in the degree that any consequence is considered likely to result from an act, just in that degree it gets moral value, for it becomes *part of the act* itself. The reason that in many cases we cannot judge of the morality of an intended act until we can judge its probable results, is that until we know of these results the action is a mere abstraction, having no content at all. *The conceived results constitute the content of the act to be performed.* They are not merely relevant to its morality, but *are* its moral quality. The question is whether any consequence is foreseen, conceived, or not. The foreseen, the *ideal* consequences are the end of the act, and as such form the *motive.*

See on Sections 6 and 7, Alexander, Moral Order and Progress, pp. 36-46; on Section 7, Green, Prolegomena to Ethics, pp. 317-323.

VIII.

Character and Conduct. We have seen that the moral sentiments, or the moral disposition (distinguished from the feelings as passing emotions), on one side, and the consequences as ideal or conceived (distinguished from the consequences that, *de facto*, result), on the other, both have moral value. If we take the moral feelings, not one by one, but as a whole, as an *attitude* of the agent toward conduct, as expressing the kind of motives which upon the whole moves him to action, we have *character.* And just so, if we take the consequences willed, not one by one, but as a whole, as the kind of end which the agent endeavors to realize, we have *conduct.* Character and conduct are, morally, the same thing, looked at first inwardly and then outwardly. Character, except as manifest in conduct, is a barren ideality. Our moral judgments are always severe upon a man who has nothing to show but 'good intentions' never executed. This is what character comes to, apart from conduct. Our only way of telling the nature of character is the conduct that issues from it. But, on the other hand, conduct is mere outward formalism, excepting as it manifests character. To say that a man's conduct is good, unless it is the manifestation of a good character, is to pass a judgment which is self-contradictory.

See Alexander, Op. cit., pp. 48-50 and p. 39.

From this point of view we are enabled to identify the two senses of motive already discussed —the ideal of action and the moving feelings. Apart from each other they are abstractions. Cæsar's motive in crossing the Rubicon may have been 'ambition,' but this was not some bare feeling. It was a feeling of ambition produced in view of the contemplation of a certain end which he wished to reach. So a boy's motive in striking a playmate may be anger, but this means (if the act is anything more than one of blind physical reaction) an anger having its conscious cause and aim, and not some abstract feeling of anger in general. The feeling which has its nature made what it is by the conceived end, and the end which has ceased to be a bare abstract conception and become an interest, are all one with each other.

Morality is then a matter pertaining to character—to the feelings and inclinations as transformed by ends of action; and to conduct—to conceived ends transformed into act under the influence of emotions. But what *kind* of character, of conduct, is right or realizes its true end? This brings us to our first problem.

PART I.

FUNDAMENTAL ETHICAL NOTIONS.

CHAPTER I.—THE GOOD.

IX.

Subdivision of Theories. We may recognize three main types of theories regarding the good, of which the first two represent (we shall attempt to show) each respectively one side of the truth, while the third combines the one-sided truths of the other two. Of the first two theories one is abstract, because it tends to find the good in the mere consequences of conduct aside from character. This is the hedonistic theory, which finds the good to be pleasure. This is either individualistic or universalistic according as it takes individual or general pleasure to be the good. The second type of theories attempts to find the good in the motive of conduct apart from consequences even as willed; it reduces the good to conformity to abstract moral law. The best type of this theory is the Kantian. We shall criticize these theories with a view to developing the factors necessary to a true moral theory.

X.

Hedonism. According to the strict hedonistic position, the pleasure resulting to the agent from his act is the end of conduct and is therefore the criterion of its morality. The position as usually taken involves, first, that pleasure is psychologically the sole motive to action; and, secondly, that the results of an act in the way of the pain or pleasure it produces are the only tests we have of the rightness of the act.

It is said above that these two points are involved in the hedonistic position as *usually* taken. They are not *necessarily* involved.

Sidgwick (Methods of Ethics, Bk. I, ch. IV and Bk. IV, ch. I) holds that pleasure is not the object of desire or motive of action, but that happiness is the moral end and criterion. On the other hand Hodgson (Theory of Practice, Vol. II, ch. II) holds that pleasure may be the motive (in the sense of impelling force) but it is never the criterion of conduct. Kant adopts the psychology of hedonism regarding pleasure as the object of desire, but holds that on that very account no object of desire can be the standard of moral conduct.

A good statement of strict individualistic hedonism is the following from Barratt, Physical Ethics, page 71: "If man aims at pleasure merely by the physical law of action, that pleasure must evidently be ultimately his own, and whether it be or not preceded by phenomena, which he calls the pain and pleasure of others, is a question not of principle but of detail, just as the force of a pound weight is unaltered whether it be composed of lead or of feathers, or whether it act directly or through pulleys."

XI.

The Hedonistic Position Supported. Hedonism holds that pleasure is both the natural end and the proper criterion of action:

The following quotation from Bentham (Principles of Morals and Legislation, Works, Vol. I, p. 1) gives a statement of both these elements. "Nature has placed man under the governance of two sovereign masters, pain and pleasure. It is for them alone to point out what we ought to do, [i. e. they are criteria] as well as to determine what we shall do [motives]. On the one hand, the standard of right or wrong [criterion]; on the other the chain of causes and effects [motives], are fastened to their throne."

1. *Pleasure as Criterion.* That the tendency of an action to produce pleasure is the standard for judging its moral value is generally held by the hedonists to be so axiomatic as to be beyond argument.

See Bain, Moral Science, p. 27. "The ultimate data must be accepted as self-evident: they have no higher authority than that mankind generally are disposed to accept them. . . Now there can be no proof offered for the position that happiness is the proper end of all human pursuits, the criterion of all right conduct. It is an ultimate or final assumption to be tested by reference to the individual judgment of mankind." So Bentham, Enquiry I, II, "The principle is not susceptible of direct proofs for that which is used to prove everything else can not itself be proved; a chain of proofs must have their commencement somewhere." Mill, Utilitarianism. (Dissertations and Discussions, pp. 348-349). "The only proof capable of being given that an object is visible is that people actually see it. In like manner the sole evidence it is possible to produce that anything is desirable is that people do actually desire it." See Stephen, Science of Ethics, p. 42; Spencer, Data of Ethics, pp. 30-32 and p. 46; Lotze, Practical Philosophy, pp. 18-19; Sidgwick, Methods of Ethics, pp. 368-369.

Hedonism, then, represents the good or the desirable and pleasure to be two names for the same fact. What indeed can be worth while unless it be either enjoyable in itself or at least a means to enjoyment? Would theft be considered bad if it resulted in pleasure or truth itself good if its universal effect were pain?

2. *Pleasure as object of desire.* It is also urged that psychological analysis shows that pleasure is not only the desirable, but also always the *desired.* Desire for an object is only a short way of saying desire for the pleasure which that object may bring. To want food is to want the pleasure it brings; to want scientific ability is to desire to find satisfaction, or attain happiness. Thus it is laid down as a general principle that the invariable object of desire, and motive of action is some pleasure to be attained; the action itself and the direct end of action being simply means to pleasure.

For a strong statement of this doctrine see Mill, Op. cit., pp. 354–5. "Desiring a thing and finding it pleasant, aversion to it and thinking of it as painful, are phenomena entirely inseparable, or rather two parts of the same phenomenon,—in strictness of language, two different modes of naming the same psychological fact; to think of an object as desirable and to think of it as pleasant are one and the same thing. See also, Bain, Emotions and Will, p. 436, Senses and Intellect, pp. 338–344; Sully, Outlines of Psychology, p. 575, "The inclination or tendency of the active mind towards what is pleasurable and away from what is painful is the essential fact in willing." Also pp. 576–577.

XII. Criticism.

Pleasure Not the End of Impulse. Taking up the points in reverse order, we shall endeavor to show first, that the motive of action, in the sense of end aimed at, is not pleasure. This point in itself, is, of course, rather psychological than ethical. Taking up then the psychology of pleasure in its connection with will, we shall discuss its relation to impulse, to desire and to motive.

It is generally agreed that the raw material of volition is found in some form or other of the impulsive or instinctive actions. Such tendencies (*e. g.*, the impulse for food, for drink, for unimpeded motion) clearly precede the reaching of an end, and hence the experience of any pleasure in the end. Our first actions, at least, are not for pleasure; on the contrary, there is an activity for some independent end, and this end being reached there is pleasure in an act which has succeeded. This suggests as a possible principle that pleasure is not so much the end of action, as an element in the activity which reaches an end. What Aristotle says of another matter is certainly true of instinctive action. "It is not true of every characteristic function that its action is attended with pleasure, *except indeed the pleasure of attaining its end.*"

See Martineau, Types of Ethical Theory, Vol. II, pp. 299–300; Sidgwick, Op. cit., pp. 38–45.

XIII. Criticism—*Continued.*

Pleasure Not the End of Desire. It may, however, be said that, while our instinctive actions have another end than pleasure, this is not true of conscious desires—that, indeed, just the difference between instinct and desire is that the former goes blindly to its end, while the latter superimposes the thought of the pleasure to be reached upon the mere instinct. So we have to analyze the nature of desire.

A child, led by impulse, has put a piece of sugar into his mouth, just as, under the same circumstances, he would put a piece of stone into his mouth. But his action results in a state of pleasure wholly unforseen by him. Now the next time the child sees the sugar he will not merely have the impulse to put it in his mouth. There will also be the remembrance of the pleasure enjoyed from sugar previously. There is consciousness of sugar as satisfying impulse and hence desire for it.

1. This is a description of an instance of desire. Does it bear us out in the doctrine that pleasure is the object of desire? It is possible that, in an irrational animal, the experience of eating food reinforces the original instinct for it with associated images of pleasure. But even this is very different from a desire for pleasure. It is simply the primordial instinct intensified and rendered more acute by new sensational factors joined to it. In the strict sense, there is still no desire, but only *stronger* impulse. Wherever there is desire there is not only a feeling of pleasure associated with other feelings (*e. g.*, those of hunger, thirst), but there is the *consciousness of an object in which satisfaction is found.* The error of the hedonistic psychology is in omitting one's consciousness of an *object* which satisfies. The hedonists are quite right in holding that the end of desire is not any object external to consciousness, but a condition of consciousness itself. The error begins in eliminating all objective (that is, active) elements from consciousness, and declaring it to be a mere state of feeling or sensation. The practical consciousness, or will, cannot be reduced to mere feeling,

any more than the theoretical consciousness, or knowledge, can be so reduced.

Even Mill, in its statement of the hedonistic psychology, does not succeed in making the object of desire mere pleasure as a state of feeling. It is the "pleasant *thing*" and not pleasure alone which he finds equivalent to the desire. It is true enough that sugar as an external fact does not awaken desire, but it is equally true that a child does not want a passive pleasure. What he wants is his own activity in which he makes the sugar his own. And it should be remembered that the case of sugar is at once a trivial and an exceptional one. Not even children want simply sweat-meats; and the larger the character which finds expression in wants, the more does the direct object of want, the bread, the meat, become a mere element in a larger system of activity. What a man wants is to live, and he wants sweet-meats, amusements, etc., just as he wants substantials—on account of their value in life.

Professor James compares the idea that pleasure is the end of desire to saying that "because no steamer can go to sea without incidentally consuming coal, . . . therefore no steamer can go to sea for any other motive than that of coal-consumption." Psychology, Vol. II, p. 558. See the entire passage, pp. 549–559.

2. But granting that an 'object' and a 'pleasure' are both necessary to desire, it may be argued

that the 'object' is ultimately a means to 'pleasure.' This expressly raises a question already incidentally touched upon: What is the controlling element in desire? Why is the object thought of as pleasant? Simply because it is thought of as satisfying want. The hedonists, says Green (Prolegomena to Ethics, p. 168), make the "mistake of supposing that a desire can be excited by the anticipation of its own satisfaction." This is to say, of course, that it exists before it exists, and thus brings itself into being.

Green, Op. cit., p. 167, states the matter thus: "Ordinary motives are interests in the attainment of objects, without which it seems to the man that he cannot satisfy himself, and in the attainment of which, *because he has desired them*, he will find a certain pleasure, but only because he has previously desired them, not because pleasures are the objects desired." Bradley says on this same point (Ethical Studies, p. 230): "The difference is between my finding my pleasure in an end, and my finding means for the end of my pleasure, and the difference is enormous." Consult the entire passage, pp. 226-235. See also Caird, Critical Philosophy of Kant, Vol. II, p. 229.

It is the object, then, which controls, and the pleasure is on account of the attaining of the desired object. But even this statement makes more division in desire than actually exists; for

3. The real object of desire is activity itself. The will takes its rise, as we have seen, in impulse; in the reaching for something to satisfy some felt

lack. Now, in reality, desire adds nothing to impulse excepting *consciousness* of the impulse. Volitional action does not differ from impulsive or instinctive, *except in bringing to consciousness the nature of the want and of the activity necessary to satisfy it.* But this makes just the difference between 'natural' or animal activity, and 'moral' or human activity. To be conscious of the impulse is to elevate it from a blind impelling force to an intended or proposed end; and thus, by bringing it *before* consciousness, both to extend its range and to idealize it, spiritualize it. To be conscious of an impulse for food means to give up the unreasoned and momentary seizing of it; to consider the relation of things to this want, what will satisfy it best, most easily, etc. The *object* of desire is not something outside the action; it is an element in the enlarged action. And as we become more and more conscious of impulse for food, we analyze our action into more and more 'objects' of desire, but these objects never become anything apart from the action itself. They are simply its analyzed and defined content. Man wants activity still, but he knows better what activity means and includes.

Thus, when we learn what the activity means, it changes its character. To the animal the activity wanted is simply that of eating the food, of realizing the momentary impulse. To man the activity becomes enlarged to include the satisfaction of a whole life, and not of one life singly, but of the family, etc., connected with the single life. The material well-being of the family becomes one of the objects of desire into which the original impulse has grown. But we misinterpret, when we conceive of this well-being as an external object lying outside the action. It means simply one aspect of the fuller action. By like growing consciousness of the meaning of the impulse, production and exchange of commodities are organized. The impulse for food is extended to include a whole range of commercial activities.

It is evident that this growing consciousness of the nature of an impulse, whereby we resolve it into manifold and comprehensive activities, also takes the impulse out of its isolation and brings it into connection with other impulses. We come to have not a series of disconnected impulses, but one all-inclusive activity in which various subordinate activities (or conscious impulses) are included. Thus, in the previous example, the impulse for food is united with the family impulse, and with the impulse for communication and intercourse with society generally. It is this growing unity with the whole range of man's action that is the 'spiritualizing' of the impulse — the natural and brutal impulse being just that which insists upon itself irrespective of all other wants. The spiritualizing of the impulse is organizing it so that it becoms one factor in action. Thus we literally come to 'eat to live', meaning by life not mere physical existence, but the whole possible sphere of active human relations.

4. Relation of activity to pleasure. We have seen that the 'object' of desire in itself is a mere abstraction; that the real object is full activity itself. We are always after larger scope of movement, fuller income in order to get larger outgo. The 'thing' is always for the sake of doing; is a part of the doing. The idea that anything less or other than life (movement, action, and doing), can satisfy man is as ridiculous when compared with the actual course of things in history, as it is false psychologically. Freedom is what we want, and freedom means full unimpeded play of interests, that is, of conscious impulses (see Sec. 34 and 51). If the object is a mere abstraction apart from activity, much more is pleasure. Mere pleasure as an object is simply the extreme of passivity, of mere having, as against action or doing. It is *possible* to make pleasure to some degree the object of desire; this is just what the voluptuary does. But it is a commonplace that the voluptuary always defeats himself. He never gets satisfaction who identifies satisfaction with having pleasures. The reason is

evident enough. Activity is what we want, and since pleasure comes from getting what we want, pleasure comes only with activity. To give up the activity, and attempt to get the pleasure is a contradiction in effect. Hence also the 'hedonistic paradox'—that in order to get pleasure we must aim at something else.

There is an interesting recognition of this in Mill himself, (see his Autobiography, p. 142). And in his Utilitarianism, in discussing the feasibility of getting happiness, he shows (pp. 318-319) that the sources of happiness are an intelligent interest in surrounding things—objects of nature, achievements of art, incidents of history—and especially an unselfish devotion to others. Which is to say that man does not find satisfaction in pleasure as such at all, but only in objective affairs—that is, in complete interpretation, in activity with a wide and full content. Further consideration of the end of desire and its relation to pleasure may be found in Green, Op. cit., pp. 123-132; pp. 163-167. Bradley, Mind, Vol. XIII, p. 1, and Dewey, Psychology, pp. 360-365.

XIV. Criticism—*Continued.*

Character and Pleasure. It now being admitted that the end of desire is activity itself in which the 'object' and 'pleasure' are simply factors, what is the moving spring to action? What is it that arouses the mind to the larger activity? Most of the hedonists have confounded the two senses of motive already spoken of, and have held that *because* pleasure is the end of desire, therefore it is the moving spring of conduct (or more often that because it is the moving spring of conduct it *therefore* is the end of desire).

Mr. Stephen (Science of Ethics, pp. 46–58), although classing himself as a hedonist, has brought out this confusion very clearly. Ordinary hedonism confounds, as he shows, the judgment of what is pleasant—the supposed end—with the pleasant judgment—the moving spring. (See also Bradley, Op. cit., pp. 232–236). It may be admitted that it is feeling which moves to action, but it is the *present* feeling which moves. If the feeling aimed at moves, it is only as through anticipation it becomes the present feeling. Now is this present feeling which moves (1) mere pleasure and (2) mere feeling at all? This introduces us to the question of the relation of pleasure (and of feeling in general) to character.

1. If the existing state of consciousness—that which moves—were pure pleasure, why should there be any movement, any act at all? The feeling which moves must be in so far complex: over against the pleasure felt in the anticipation of an end as satisfying, there must be pain felt in the contrasting unsatisfactory present condition. There must be tension between the anticipated or ideal action, and the actual or present (relative) non-action. And it is this tension, in which pain is just

as normal an element as pleasure, which moves. Desire is just this tension of an action which satisfies, and yet is only ideal, against an actual possession which, in contrast with the ideal action, is felt as incomplete action, or lack, and hence as unsatisfactory.

2. The question now comes as to the nature of this tension. We may call it 'feeling,' if we will, and say that feeling is the sole motive power to action. But there is no such thing as feeling at large, and the important thing, morally, is what *kind* of feeling moves. To take a mere abstraction like 'feeling' for the source of action is, at root, the fallacy of hedonism. To raise the question, What is it that makes the feeling what it is, is to recognize that the feeling, taken concretely, is *character* in a certain attitude.

Stephen, who has insisted with great force that feeling is the sole 'motive' to action, has yet shown with equal cogency the moral uselessness of such a doctrine, when feeling is left undefined (Op. cit., p. 44). "The love of happiness must express the sole possible motive of Judas Iscariot and his master; it must explain the conduct of Stylites on his column, of Tiberius at Capreæ, of A Kempis in his cell, and of Nelson in the cockpit of the Victory. It must be equally good for saints, martyrs, heroes, cowards, debauchees, ascetics, mystics, cynics, misers, prodigals, men, women, and babes in arms." Surely, this is only to say, in effect, that 'love of happiness' is a pure bit of scholasticism, an undefined entity.

In a hedonistic argument (by Stanton Coit, Mind, Vol. XI, p. 349), the fallacy is seen in the following discussion. The story is told of Abraham Lincoln that he once passed an animal in distress by the side of the road, and that, after going by, he finally went back and got him out of the ditch. On being praised for his act, he replied that he did it on his own account, since he kept getting more uncomfortable as he thought of the animal in distress. From this, it cannot be inferred that love of pleasure is at the basis of moral acts. The mere lumping off of feeling as the spring of conduct overlooks the only important thing morally—the fact that Lincoln felt pain at the thought of the animal unrelieved, and pleasure at the idea of its relief, just because he was a man of compassionate *character*. It was not the feeling, but the character revealed in, and creative of, the feeling that was the real source of the act.

To connect this with our previous account of desire (p. 26): the important thing morally is that the nature of the tension between fact and idea—the actual state and the ideal activity—is an expression of character. What kind of activity does it take to satisfy a man? Does riding in a comfortable carriage, and following the course of his own reflections exhaust his need of action? or does his full activity require that note be taken of a suffering animal? It is the kind of character one is (that is, the kind of activity which satisfies and expresses one) which decides what pleasure shall be taken in an anticipated end, what feeling of lack or hindrance (what pain) there shall be in the given state, and hence what the resulting tension, or desire, shall be. It is, therefore, character which moves to conduct.

Mere wishing, the mere floating fancy of this or that thing as desirable, is not desire. To *want* is an active projection of character; really and deeply to want is no surface and passing feeling; it is the stirring of character to its depths. There may be repressed activity; that is not, of itself, desire. There may be an image of larger activity; that is not, of itself, desire. But given the *consciousness* of a repressed activity in view of the perception of a possible larger action, and a man strives within himself to break his bonds and reach the new satisfaction. This striving within one's self, before the activity becomes overt, is the emotional antecedent of action. But this inward striving or tension, which constitutes desire, is so far from being *mere* emotion that it is character itself—character as it turns an inward or ideal advance into an outward, or real progress, into action.

We may fall back on Aristotle's statement (page 38, of Peters' translation of his ethics): "The pleasure or pain that accompanies an act must be regarded as a *test of character*. He who abstains from the pleasures of the body and rejoices in his abstinence is temperate, while he who is vexed at having to abstain is still profligate. As Plato tells us, man needs to be so trained from youth up as to take pleasure and pain *in the right objects*."

XV.

Summary. The truth in hedonism is its conviction that the good, the end of man, is not to be found in any outward object, but only in what comes home to man in his own conscious experience. The error is in reducing this experience to mere having, to bare feelings or affections, eliminating the element of doing. It is this doing which satisfies man, and it is this which involves as its content (as knowledge of impulse, instead of blind impulse) objective and permanent ends. When Mill speaks of the end of desire as a "satisfied life," (p. 317 of Utilitarianism) he carries our assent; but to reduce this satisfied life to feelings of pleasure, and absence of pains, is to destroy the life and hence the satisfaction. As Mill recognizes, a life bounded by the agent's own feelings would be, as of course, a life "centred in his own miserable individuality." (Mill, p. 319). Such words have meaning only because they suggest the contrast with activity in which are comprehended, as 'ends' or 'objects' (that is, as part of its defined content) things—art, science and industry—and persons (see Secs. 34 and 35).

Here too we must 'back to Aristotle.' According to him the end of conduct is *eudaimonia*, success, welfare, satisfied life. But *eudaimonia* is found not in pleasure, but in the fulfillment of human powers and functions, in which fulfillment, since it is fulfillment, pleasure is had. (Ethics, Bk. I, ch. 4-8).

We now take up the question whether pleasure is a standard of right action, having finished the discussion concerning it as an end of desire.

XVI.

Pleasure as the Standard of Conduct.

The line of criticism on this point may be stated as follows: Pleasure fails as a standard for the very reason that it fails as a motive. Pleasure, *as conceived by the hedonist*, is passive, merely agreeable sensations, without any objective and qualitative (active) character. This being so, there is no permanent, fixed basis to which we may refer *acts* and by which we may judge them. A standard implies a single comprehensive end which unifies all acts and through connection with which each gets its moral value fixed. Only action can be a standard for acts. To reduce all acts to means to getting a mere state of feeling is the inevitable consequence of hedonism. So reducing them is to deprive them of any standard of value.

An end to serve as standard must be (1) a comprehensive end for all the acts of an individual, and (2) an end comprehending the activities of various individuals—a common good.

1. The moral end must be that for the sake of which all conduct occurs—the *organizing principle* of conduct—a totality, a system. If pleasure is the end it is because each detail of conduct gets its placing, its moral value through relation to pleasure, through the contribution it makes to pleasure.

2. The moral end must also include the ends of the various agents who make up society. It must be capable of constituting a social system out of the acts of various agents, as well as an individual system out of the various acts of one agent; or, more simply, the moral end must be not only the good for all the particular acts of an individual, but must be a *common good*—a good which in satisfying one, satisfies others.

All ethical theories would claim that the end proposed by them served these two purposes. We shall endeavor to show that the hedonistic theory, the doctrine that the pleasure is the good, is not capable of serving either of them.

XVII.

Pleasure Not a Standard.

1. *It does not unify character.* In the first place, the hedonistic theory makes an unreal and impossible separation between conduct and character. The psy-

chology of hedonism comes into conflict with its ethics. According to the former the motive of all action is to secure pleasure or avoid pain. So far as the motive is concerned, on this theory there can be no immoral action at all. That the agent should not be moved by pleasure, and by what, at the time of acting, is the greatest pleasure possible, would be a psychological impossibility. Every motive would be good, or rather there would be no distinction of good or bad pertaining to the motive. The character of the agent, as measured by his motives, could never, under such circumstances, have any moral quality.

To the consequences of action, or the conduct proper, however, the terms good and bad might be applied. Although the agent is moved by pleasurable feelings, the result of his action may be painful and thus bad. In a word, on the hedonistic theory, it is only the external consequences of conduct, or conduct divorced from character, to which moral adjectives have any application. Such a separation not only contradicts our experience (see VIII), but inverts the true order of moral judgment. Consequences do not enter into the moral estimate at all, except so far as, being foreseen, they are the act in idea. That is, it is only as the consequences are taken up into the motive, and thus related to character, that they are subject to moral judgment.

Indeed, except so far as action expresses character, it is not conduct, but mere physical sequence, as irrelevant to morality as the change in blood distribution, which also is the 'result' of an action. Hedonism has to rule out at the start the only thing that gives totality to action—the character of the agent, or conduct as the outcome of motives. Furthermore, the ordinary judgment of men, instead of saying that the sole moral motive is to get pleasure, would say that to reduce everything to means for getting pleasure is the very essence of immorality.

On the point above, compare Bentham, Op. cit., I, p. 48. "A motive is substantially nothing more than pleasure or pain operating in a certain manner. Now pleasure is in itself a good: nay, even, setting aside immunity from pain, the only good; pain is in itself an evil, and, indeed, without exception, the only evil; or else the words good and evil have no meaning. And this is alike true of every sort of pain and of every sort of pleasure. It follows, therefore, immediately and incontestably, that there is no such thing as any sort of motive that is in itself a bad one. If motives are good or bad, it is only on account of their effects; good on account of their tendency to produce pleasure or avert pain; bad on account of their tendency to produce pain or avert pleasure. Now the case is, that from one and the same motive, and from every kind of motive, may proceed actions that are good, others that are bad and others that are indifferent." Further, on p. 60, Bentham asks: "Is there nothing, then, about a man that can properly be termed good or bad, when on such or such an occasion he suffers himself to be governed by such or such a motive? Yes, certainly, his *disposition*. Now disposition is a kind of fictitious entity, feigned for the convenience of discourse, in order to express what there is supposed to be *permanent* in a man's frame of mind. It is with disposition as with everything else; it will be good or bad according to its effects." The first quotation, it will be noticed, simply states that the motive is in itself always good, while conduct (*i. e.*, consequences) may be good, bad or indifferent. The second quotation seems, however, to pass moral judgment upon character under the name of disposition. But disposition is judged according to the tendency of a person's actions. A good or bad disposition, here, can mean nothing intrinsic to the person, but only that the person has been observed to act in ways that usually produce pain or pleasure, as the case may be. The term is a 'fiction', and is a backhanded way of expressing a somewhat habitual *result* of a given person's conduct his motive remaining good (or for pleasure) all the time. The agent would never pronounce any such judgment upon his own disposition, unless as a sort of suprise that, his motive being 'good,' his actions turn out so 'bad' all the time. At most, the judgment regarding disposition is a sort of label put upon a man by others, a label of "Look out for him, he is dangerous," or, "Behold, a helpful man."

The moral standard of hedonism does not, then, bear any relation to the character of the agent, does not enable us to judge it, either as a whole or in any specific manifestation.

XVIII.

It Does Not Give a Criterion for Concrete Acts. Pleasure, as the end, fails also to throw light on the moral value of any specific acts. Its failure in this respect is, indeed, only the other side of that just spoken of. There is no organizing principle, no 'universal' on the basis of which various acts fall into a system or order. The moral life is left a series of shreds and patches, where each act is torn off, as to its moral value, from every other. Each act is right or wrong, according as *it* gives pleasure or pain, and independently of any whole of life. There is, indeed, no whole of moral life at all, but only a series of isolated, disconnected acts. Possession, passivity, *mere* feeling, by its very nature cannot unite—each feeling is itself and that is the end of it. It is action which reduces multiplicity to unity. We cannot say, in the hedonistic theory, that pleasure is the end, but *pleasures.*

Each act stands by itself—the only question is: What pleasure will *it* give? The settling of this question is the "hedonistic calculus." We must discover the intensity, duration, certainty, degree of nearness of the pleasure likely to arise from the given act, and also its purity, or likelihood of being accompanied by secondary pains and pleasures. Then we are to strike the balance between the respective sums on the pleasure and pain sides, and, according as this balance is one of pleasure or pain, the act is good or evil.

Bentham, Op. cit., p. 16, was the first to go into detail as to this method. He has also given certain memoriter verses stating "the points on which the whole fabric of morals and legislation may be seen to rest.

Intense, long, certain, speedy, fruitful, pure,
Such marks in pleasures and in pains endure,
Such pleasures seek, if private be thy end.
If it be public, wide let them extend.
Such pains avoid whichever be thy view,
If pains must come, let them extend to few."

This, however, in its reference to others, states the utilitarian as well as the hedonistic view.

Now, it must be remembered that, if pleasure is the end, there is no intrinsic connection between the motive of the act, and its result. It is not claimed that there is anything belonging intrinsically to the motive of the act which makes it result in pleasure or pain. To make such a claim would be to declare the moral quality of the act the criterion of the pleasure, instead of pleasure the criterion of the act. The pleasures are external to the act; they are irrelevant and accidental to its quality. There is no 'universal,' no intrinsic bond of connection between the act and its consequences. The consequence is a mere particular state of feeling, which, in this instance, the act has happened to bring about.

More concretely, this act of truth-telling has in this instance, brought about pleasure. Shall we call it right? Right in *this* instance, of course; but is it right generally? Is truth-telling, as such, right, or is it merely that this instance of it happens to be right? Evidently, on the hedonistic basis, we cannot get beyond the latter judgment. *Prior* to any act, there will be plenty of difficulties in telling whether it, as *particular*, is right or wrong. The consequences depend not merely on the result intended, but upon a multitude of circumstances outside of the foresight and control of the agent. And there can be only a precarious calculation of possibilities and probabilities — a method which would always favor laxity of conduct in all but the the most conscientious of men, and which would throw the conscientious into uncertainty and perplexity in the degree of their conscientiousness.

"If once the pleas of instinct are to be abolished and replaced by a hedonistic arithmetic, the whole realm of animated nature has to be reckoned with in weaving the tissue of moral relations, and the problem becomes infinite and insoluble".—Martineau, Op. cit., Vol. II, p. 334.

But waive this; let the particular case be settled. There is still no law, no principle, indeed no presumption as to future conduct. The act is not right *because* it is *truth-telling*, but because, in this instance, cicumstances were such as to throw a balance of pleasure in its favor. This establishes no certainty, no probability as to its next outcome. The result *then* will depend wholly upon circumstances existing *then*—circumstances which have no intrinsic relation to the act and which must change from time to time.

The hedonist would escape this abolition of all principle, or even rule, by falling back upon a number of cases—'past experience' it is called. We have found in a number of cases that a certain procedure has resulted in pleasure, and this result is sufficient to guide us in a vast number of cases which come up.

Says Mill (Op. cit., pp. 332–4): "During the whole past duration of the species, mankind have been learning by experience the tendencies of actions, on which experience all the prudence as well as all the morality of life are dependent. . . . . Mankind must by this time have acquired positive belief as to the effects of some actions on their happiness; and the beliefs which have thus come down are the rules of morality for the multitude, and for the philosopher, until he has succeeded in finding better. . . . . Nobody argues that the art of navigation is not founded on astronomy, because sailors cannot wait to calculate the 'Nautical Almanac'. Being rational creatures, they go to sea with it ready calculated; and all rational creatures go out upon the sea of life with their minds made up on the common questions of right and wrong, as well as on many of the far more difficult questions of wise and foolish."

That we do learn from experience the moral nature of actions is undoubted. The only question is: *if* hedonism were true, *could* we so learn? Suppose that I were convinced that the results of murder in the past had been generally, or even without exception (though this could not be proved), painful; as long as the act and the result in the way of feeling (pain or pleasure) are conceived as having no intrinsic connection, this would not prove that in the present instance murder will give a surplus of pain. I am not thinking of committing murder in general, but of murder under certain specific present circumstances. These circumstances may, and, to some extent, *must* vary from all previous instances of murder. How then can I reason from them to it? Or, rather, let me use the previous cases as much as I may, the moral quality of the act I am now to perform must still be judged not from them, but from the circumstances of the present case. To judge otherwise, is, on hedonistic principles, to be careless, perhaps criminally careless as to one's conduct. The more convinced a man is of the truth of hedonism and the more conscientious he is, the more he is bound *not* to be guided by previous circumstances, but to form his judgment anew concerning the new case. This result flows out of the very nature of the hedonistic ideal. Pleasure is not an activity, but simply a particular feeling, enduring only while it is felt. Moreover, there is in it no principle which connects it intrinsically with any *kind* of action. To suppose then that, because ninety-nine cases of murder have resulted in pain, the hundredth will, is on a par with reasoning that because ninety-nine days have been frosty, the hundredth will be. Each case, taken as particular, must be decided wholly by itself. There is no continuous moral life, and no system of conduct. There is only a succession of unlike acts.

Mill, in his examination of Whewell, (Diss. and Diss., Vol. III, pp. 158-59), tries to establish a general principle, if not a universal law, by arguing that, even in exceptional cases, the agent is bound to respect the rule, because to act otherwise would weaken the rule, and thus lead to its being disregarded in other cases, in which its observance results in pleasure. There are, he says, persons so wicked that their removal from the earth would undoubtedly increase the sum total of happiness. But if persons were to violate the general rule in these cases, it would tend to destroy the rule. "If it were thought allowable for any one to put to death at pleasure any human being whom he believes that the world would be well rid of,—nobody's life would be safe." That is to say, if every one were really to act upon and carry out the hedonistic principle, no rule of life would exist. This does very well as a *reductio ad absurdum* of hedonism, or as an argument against adopting hedonism, but it is difficult to see how Mill thought that it established a 'rule' on a hedonistic basis. Mill's argument comes to saying that if hedonism were uniformly acted upon, it would defeat itself—that is, pleasure would not result. Therefore, in order to get pleasure, we must not act upon the principle of hedonism at all, but follow a general rule. Otherwise put: hedonism gives no general rule, but we must have a general rule to make hedonism work; and therefore there is a general rule! This begging of the question comes out even more plainly as Mill goes on: "If one person may break through the rule on his own judgment, the same liberty cannot be refused to others; and, since no one could rely on the rule's being observed, the rule would cease to exist." All of this is obviously true, but it amounts to saying: "We *must* have a rule, and this we would not have if we carried out the hedonistic principle in each case; therefore, we must not carry it out." A principle, that carried out destroys all rules which pretend to rest upon it, lays itself open to suspicion. Mill assumes the entire question in assuming that there is a rule. Grant this, and the necessity of not 'making exceptions,' that is, of not applying the hedonistic standard to each case, on its own merits, follows. But the argument which Mill needs to meet is that hedonism *requires* us to apply the standard to each case in itself, and that, therefore, there *is* no rule. Mill simply says —*assume* the rule, and it follows, etc.

See Bradley, Op. cit., pp. 96-101; Green, Bk. IV, Ch. 3; Martineau, Vol. II, pp. 329-334.

XIX.

The Sum and the Quality of Pleasure as the Standard. We have been dealing with hedonism in its strict form—that which makes *a* pleasure, considered as to its intensity, certainty, etc., the end of an act. Hedonism in this form fails to unify life, and fails, therefore, to supply any standard. But the end of conduct is often stated to be the greatest possible sum of pleasnres, thus introducing a certain element of generality. Mill goes further and brings in the idea of quality of pleasure.

Regarding the sum of pleasures the following from Sidgwick (Op. cit. p. 382; see also p. 114) gives the hedonistic statement. "The assumption is involved that all pleasures are capable of being compared qualitatively with one another and with all pains; that every feeling has a certain intensive quality, positive or negative (or perhaps zero) in respect to its desirableness and that the quantity may be known, so that each may be weighed in ethical scales against any other. This assumption is involved in the very motion of maximum happiness," as the attempt to make "as great as possible a sum of elements not quantitatively commensurable would be a mathematical absurdity."

I. Sum of pleasures as the moral end. This, first, taken as criterion, comes into conflict with the hedonistic psychology of pleasure as the motive of acts; and, secondly, it requires some objective standard by means of which pleasure is to be summed, and is, in so far, a surrender of the whole hedonistic position.

1. If the object of desire is pleasure or a state of feeling which exists only as it is felt, it is impossible that we should desire a greatest sum of pleasures. We can desire a pleasure and that only. It is not even possible that we should ever desire a continuous series of pleasures. We can desire one pleasure and when that is gone, another, but we can not unify our desires enough to aim at even a sum of pleasures.

This is well put by Green (Op. cit. p. 236). "For the feeling of a pleased person, or in relation to his sense of enjoyment, pleasure cannot form a sum. However numerous the sources of a state of pleasant feeling, it is one and is over before another can be enjoyed. It and its successors can be added together in thought, but not in enjoyment or in imagination of an enjoyment. If the desire is only for pleasure, *i. e.*, for an enjoyment or feeling of pleasure, we are simply victims of words when we talk of desire for a sum of pleasures, much more when we take the greatest imaginable sum to be the most desirable." See the whole passage, pp. 235-246.

2. But the phrase "sum of pleasures" undoubtedly has a meaning—though the fact that it has a meaning shows the untruth of the hedonistic psychology. Surrendering this psychology, what shall we say of the maximum possibility of pleasure as the criterion of the morality of acts? It must be conceded that this conception does afford some basis—although a rather slippery one—for the unification of conduct. Each act is considered now not in its isolation merely, but in its connection with other acts, according as its relation to them may increase or decrease the possible sum of future happiness. But this very fact that some universal, or element of relation, albeit a quantitative one, has been introduced, arouses this inquiry: Whence do we derive it? How do we get the thought of a sum of pleasure, and of a maximum sum? *Only by taking into account the objective conditions upon which pleasures depend, and by judging the pleasures from the*

standpoint of these objective conditions. When we imagine we are thinking of a sum of pleasures, we are really thinking of that totality of conditions which will come nearest affording us self-satisfaction—we are thinking of a comprehensive and continuous activity whose various parts are adjusted to one another. Because it is complete activity, it is necessarily conceived as giving the greatest possible pleasure, but apart from reference to complete activity and apart from the objects in which this is realized, the phrase 'greatest sum of happiness' is a mere phrase. Pleasures must be measured by a standard, by a yard stick, before they can be summed in thought, and the yard stick we use is the activity in which the pleasure comes. We do not measure conduct by pleasure, but we compare and sum up pleasures on the basis of the objects which occasion them. To add feelings, mere transitory consequences, without first reducing those feelings to a common denominator by their relation to one objective standard, is an impossibility. Pleasure is a sort of sign or symbol of the object which satisfies, and we may carry on our judgment, if we will, in terms of the sign, without reference to the standard, but to argue as if the sign were the thing, as if the sum of pleasure were the activity, is suicidal.

Thus Green says (Op. cit., p. 244): "In truth a man's reference to his own true happiness is a reference to the objects which chiefly interest him, and has its controlling power on that account. More strictly, it is a reference to an ideal state of well-being, a state in which he shall be satisfied; *but the objects of the man's chief interests supply the filling of that ideal state.*" See the argument as put by Alexander (Moral Order and Progress, pp. 199-200). Alexander has also brought out (Ibid, pp. 207–210) that even if we are going to use a quantitative standard, the idea of a sum is not a very happy one. It is not so much a sum of pleasures we want, as a certain proportionate distribution and combination of pleasures. "To regard the greatest sum of pleasures as the test of conduct, supposing that we could express it in units of pleasure, would be like declaring that when you had an atomic weight of 98 you had sulphuric acid. The numerical test would be useless unless we knew what elements were to be combined, and in what proportion. Similarly till we know what kinds of activities (and therefore what kinds of pleasures) go with one another to form the end, the greatest sum of pleasures will give us only the equivalent of the end, but will not tell us what the composition of the end is, still less how to get at it; or, to put the matter more simply, when we know what the characters of persons are, and how they are combined in morality, we then estimate the corresponding sum of pleasures." (p. 209.)

II. A certain quality of pleasure the end. Some moralists, notably John Stuart Mill, introduce considerations regarding the quality of pleasure into the conception of the end. "It is quite compatible," says Mill, "with the principle of utility to recognize the fact that some kinds of pleasure are more desirable and more valuable than others." (p. 310.) Is it compatible? Is kind of pleasure the same thing as pleasure? does not strict hedonism demand that all kinds of pleasure equally present as to intensity in consciousness shall be of the same value? To say otherwise is to give up pleasure as such as the standard and to hold that we have means for discriminating the respective values of pleasures which simply, *as feelings*, are the same. It is to hold, that is to say, that there is some standard of value external to the pleasures as such, by means of which their moral quality may be judged. In this case, this independent standard is the real moral criterion which we are employing. Hedonism is surrendered.

Kant's position on this point seems impregnable. "It is surprising," he says, "that men otherwise astute can think it possible to distinguish between higher and lower desires, according as the ideas which are connected with the feeling of pleasure have their origin in the senses or in the understanding; for when we inquire what are the determining grounds of desire, and place them in some expected pleasantness, it is of no consequence whence the *idea* of this pleasing object is derived, but only how much it *pleases*. . . . . The only thing that concerns one, in order to decide choice, is how great, how long continued, how easily obtained and how often repeated, this agreeableness is For as to the man who wants money to spend, it is all the same whether the gold was dug out of the mountain or washed out of the sand, provided it is everywhere accepted at the same value; so the man who cares only for the enjoyment of life does not ask whether the ideas are of the understanding or the senses, but only *how much* and *how great pleasure* they will give for the longest time."

See also Bradley, Op. cit., pp. 105-110.

When we ask how the differences in quality are established and how we translate this qualitative difference into moral difference, the surrender of pleasure as the standard becomes even more evident. We must know not only the fact of different qualities, but how to decide which is 'higher' than any other. We must bring the qualities before a tribunal of judgment which applies to them some standard of measurement. In themselves qualities may be different, but they are not higher and lower. What is the tribunal and what is the law of judgment? According to Mill the tribunal is the preference of those who are acquainted with both kinds of pleasure.

"Of two pleasures, if there be one to which all, or almost all who have experience of both, give a decided preference, irrespective of any feeling of moral obligation to prefer it, that is the more desirable pleasure." It is an unquestionable fact that such differences exist. "Few human creatures would consent to be changed into any of the lower animals for a promise of the fullest allowance of a beast's pleasures. No intelligent person would consent to be a fool; no instructed person would be an ignoramus; no person of feeling and conscience would be selfish and base, even though they should be persuaded that the fool, the dunce or the rascal is better satisfied with his lot than they are with theirs. . . . . It is better to be a human being dissatisfied, than a pig satisfied; better to be a Socrates dissatisfied, than a fool satisfied. And if the fool or the pig are of a different opinion, it is because they only know their own side of the question. The other party to the comparison knows both sides."—Mill, Op. cit., pp. 311-313. And in an omitted portion Mill says the reason that one of the higher faculty would prefer a suffering which goes along with that higher capacity, to more pleasure on a lower plane, is something of which "the most appropriate appellation is a sense of dignity, which all human beings possess in one form or another."

A question immediately arises regarding this standard of preferability. Is it the mere historical fact that some man, who has experienced both, prefers A to B that makes A more desirable? Surely I might say that if that person prefers A, A is more desirable to him, but that I for my part prefer B, and that I do not intend to give up my preference. And why should I, even though thousands of other men happened to prefer A? B is the greater pleasure, none the less, to me, and as a hedonist I must cling to the only standard that I have. The hedonists, in a word, have appealed to feeling, and to feeling they must go for judgment. And feeling exists only as it is felt and only to him who feels it.

On the other hand, perhaps it is not the bare fact that some men prefer one pleasure to another that makes it more desirable, but something in the character of the men who prefer. And this is what Mill implies. It is a "sense of dignity" belonging to man which makes his judgment of pleasure better than that of animals; it is the human being against the pig, Socrates against the fool, the good man against the rascal. This is the complete surrender of hedonism, and the all but explicit assertion that human character, goodness, wisdom, are the criteria of pleasure, instead of pleasure the criterion of character and goodness. Mill's "sense of dignity," which is to be considered in all estimates of pleasures, is just the sense of a moral (or active) capacity and destiny belonging to man. To refer pleasures to *this* is to make it the standard, and with this standard the anti-hedonist may well be content, while asking, however, for its further analysis.

To sum up our long discussion of pleasure as a criterion of conduct in respect of its unity, we may say: Pleasure, *as it actually exists in man*, may be taken as *a* criterion, although not the really primary one, of action. But this is not hedonism; for pleasure as it *exists* is something more than pleasurable feeling; it is qualified through and through by the kind of action which it accompanies, by the kind of objects which the activity comprehends. And thus it is always a secondary criterion. The moment we begin to analyze we must ask what *kind of activity*, what kind of object it is which the pleasure accompanies and of which it is a symbol. We may, if we will, calculate a man's wealth in terms of dollars and cents; but this is only because we can translate the money, the symbol, into goods, the reality. To desire pleasure instead of an activity of self, is to substitute symbol for fact, and a symbol cut off from fact ceases to be a symbol. Pleasure, as the hedonist treats it, mere agreeable feeling without active and thus objective relationships, is wholly an abstraction. Since an abstraction, to make it the end of desire results in self-contradiction; while to make it the standard of conduct is to deprive life of all unity, all system, in a word—of all standard.

XX.

The Failure of Pleasure as a Standard to Unify Conduct Socially.

Thus far our examination of the hedonistic criterion has been devoted to showing that it will not make a system out of individual conduct. We have now to recognize the fact that pleasure is not a common good, and therefore fails to give a social unity to conduct—that is, it does not offer an end for which men may coöperate, or a good which reached by one must be shared by another. No argument is needed to show, theoretically, that any proposed moral criterion must, in order to be valid, harmonize the interests and activities of different men, or to show, practically, that the whole tendency of the modern democratic and philanthropic movement has been to discover and realize a good in which men shall share on the basis of an equal principle. It is contended that hedonism fails to satisfy these needs. According to it, the end for each man is his own pleasure. Pleasure is nothing objective in which men may equally participate. It is purely individual in the most exclusive sense of that term. It is a state of feeling and can be enjoyed only while felt, and only by the one who feels it. To set it up for the ideal of conduct is to turn life into an exclusive and excluding struggle for possession of the means of personal enjoyment; it is to erect into a principle the idea of the war of all against all. No end more thoroughly disintegrating than individual agreeable sensation could well be imagined.

Says Kant, (page 116 of Abbott's Trans., entitled Kant's Theory of Ethics) on the basis of the desire of happiness "there results a harmony like that which a certain satirical poem depicts as existing between a married couple bent on going to ruin: O, marvellous harmony, what he wishes, she wishes also; or like what is said of the pledge of Francis I to the emperor Charles V, what my brother Charles wishes that I wish also (*viz.*, Milan)."

Almost all modern moralists who take pleasure as the end conceive it to be not individual pleasure, but the happiness of all men or even of all sentient creatures. Thus we are brought to the consideration of Utilitarianism.

Says Mill (Op. cit., p. 323), "The happiness which forms the Utilitarian standard of what is right in conduct is not the agent's own happiness, but that of all concerned; as between his own happiness and that of others, Utilitarianism requires him to be as strictly impartial as a disinterested and benevolent spectator." And (page 315) the Utilitarian standard is "not the agent's own greatest happiness, but the greatest amount of happiness altogether." See also Sidgwick (Op. cit., p. 379), "By Utilitarianism is here meant the ethical theory, first distinctly formulated by Bentham, that the conduct which, under any given circumstances is externally or objectively right is that which will produce the greatest amount of happiness *on the whole;* that is, taking into account all whose happiness is affected by the conduct. It would tend to clearness if we might call this principle, and the method based upon it, by some such name as Universalistic hedonism." As popularly put, the utilitarian standard is the "greatest happiness of the greatest number." While in its calculation "each is to count for one and only one." (*Bentham*). And finally Bain (Emotions and Mill, p. 303), "Utility is opposed to the selfish theory, for, as propounded, it always implies the good of society generally, and the subordination of individual interests to the general good."

XXI.

Criticism of Utilitarianism. The utilitarian theory certainly does away entirely with one of the two main objections to hedonism—its failure to provide a general, as distinct from a private end. The question which we have to meet, however, is whether this extension of the end from the individual to society is consistent with the fundamental principles of hedonism. *How* do we get from individual pleasure to the happiness of all?

An intuitional utilitarian, like Sidgwick, has ready an answer which is not open to the empirical utilitarians, like Bentham, Mill and Bain. Methods of Ethics, Bk. III, ch. 13-14, p. 355. "We may obtain the *self-evident principle* that the good of any one individual is of no more importance, as a part of universal good, than the good of any other. The abstract principle of the duty of benevolence, *so far as it is cognizable by direct intuition*" is, "that one is morally bound to regard the good of any other individual as much as one's own"—and page 364, "*the principles, so far as they are immediately known by abstract intuition*, can only be stated as precepts to seek (1) one's own good on the whole, and (2) the good of any other no less than one's own, in so far as it is no less an element of universal good." Sidgwick, that is, differs in two important points from most utilitarians. He holds that pleasure is not the sole, or even the usual object of desire. And he holds that we have an immediate faculty of rational intuition which informs us that the good of others is as desirable an end of our conduct as is our own happiness. Our former arguments against pleasure as the *end*, bear, of course, equally against this theory, but not the following arguments. Criticisms of this position of Sidgwick's will be found in Green (Op. cit., pp. 406-415); Bradley (Op. cit., pp. 114-117).

The popular answer to the question how we get from individual to general happiness, misses the entire point of the question. This answer simply says that happiness is '*intrinsically* desirable'. Let it be so; but 'happiness' in this general way is a mere abstraction. Happiness is always a particular condition of one particular person. Whose happiness is desirable and *to whom?* Because my happiness is intrinsically desirable to me, does it follow that your happiness is intrinsically desirable to me? Indeed, in the hedonistic psychology, is it not nonsense to say that a state of your feeling is desirable to me? Mill's amplified version of the popular answer brings out the ambiguity all the more plainly. He says (Utilitarianism, p. 349), "No reason can be given why the general happiness is desirable, except that each person, so far as he believes it to be obtainable, desires his own happiness. This, however, being a fact, we have not only all the proof which the case admits of, but all which it is possible to require, that happiness is a good; that each person's happiness is a good to that person; and the general happiness, therefore, a good to the aggregate of all persons." But does it follow that because the happiness of A is an end to A, the happiness of B an end to B, and the happiness of C an end to C, that, therefore, the happiness of B and C is an end to A? There is obviously no connection between the premises and the supposed conclusion. And there appears to be, as Mill puts it, only an account of the ambiguity of his last clause, "the general happiness a good to the aggregate of all persons." The good of A and B and C may be a good to the aggregate (A + B + C), but what universalistic hedonism requires is that the aggregate good of A + B + C, be a good to A and to B and to C taken separately —a very different proposition. Mill is guilty of the fallacy known logically as the fallacy of division—arguing from a collective whole to the distributed units. Because all men want to be happy, it hardly follows that every man wants all to be happy. There is, accordingly, no *direct* road from individualistic hedonism—private pleasure—to universalistic—general pleasure. Moreover, if we adopt the usual psychology of hedonism and say that pleasure is the motive of acting, it is absolutely absurd to say that general pleasure can be a motive. How can I be moved by the happiness which exists in some one else? I may feel a pleasure resembling his, and be moved by it, but that is quite a different matter.

XXII.

Indirect Means of Identifying Private and General Pleasure.

Is there any *indirect* method of going from the pleasure of one to the pleasure of all? Upon the whole, the utilitarians do not claim that there is any natural and immediate connection between the desire for private and for general happiness, but suppose that there are certain means which are instrumental in bringing about an identity. Of these means the sympathetic emotions and the influence of law and of education are the chief. Each of these, moreover, coöperates with the other.

1. *Sympathetic and Social Emotions.*

We are so constituted by nature that we take pleasure in the happiness of others and feel pain in their misery. A proper regard for our own welfare must lead us, therefore, to take an interest in the pleasure of others. Our own feelings, moreover, are largely influenced by the feelings of others toward us. If we act in a certain way we shall incur the disapprobation of others, and this, independently of any overt punishment it may lead them to inflict upon us, arouses feelings of shame, of inferiority, of being under the displeasure of others, feelings all of which are decidedly painful. The more enlightened our judgment, the more we see how our pleasures are bound up in those of others.

"The Dictates of Utility" (Bentham, Op. cit., p. 56) are neither more nor less than the dictates of the most extensive and enlightened (that is, well advised) benevolence," and (p. 18), "The pleasures of benevolence are the pleasures resulting from the view of any pleasures supposed to be possessed by the beings who may be the objects of benevolence. . . . . These may also be called the pleasures of good will, the pleasures of sympathy, or the pleasures of the benevolent or social affections"; and (p. 144), "What motives (independent of such as legislation and religion may choose to furnish) can one man have to consult the happiness of another? . . . . In answer to this, it cannot but be admitted that the only interests which a man at all times and upon all occasions is sure to find *adequate* motives for consulting, are his own. Notwithstanding this, there are no occasions in which a man has not some motives for consulting the happiness of other men. In the first place he has, on all occasions, the purely social motive of sympathy and benevolence; in the next place he has, on most occasions, the semi-social motives of love of amity and love of reputation." And so in the Deontology, which, however, was not published by Bentham himself, page 203, "The more enlightened one is, the more one forms the habit of general benevolence, because it is seen that the interests of men combine with each other in more points than they conflict in."

2. *Education and Law.*

Education, working directly and internally upon the feelings, and government, appealing to them from without through commands and penalties, are constantly effecting an increasing identity of self-interest and regard for others. These means supplement the action of sympathy and the more instinctive emotions. They stimulate and even induce a proper interest in the pleasures of others. In governmental law, with its punishments, we have an express instrument for making the pleasures of one harmonize with (or at least not conflict with) the pleasures of others.

Thus Bentham, after stating that an enlightened mind perceives the identity of self-interest and that of others (or of *egoism* and *altruism*, as these interests are now commonly called), goes on (Deontology, p. 201): "The majority do not have sufficient enlightenment, nor enough moral feeling so that their character goes beyond the aid of laws, and so the legislator should supplement the frailty of this natural interest, in adding to it an artificial interest more appreciable and more continuous. Thus the government augments and extends the connexion which exists between prudence and benevolence." Mill says (Op. cit., p. 323): "To do as you would be done by, and to love your neighbor as yourself, constitute the ideal perfection of utilitarian morality. As the means of making the nearest approach to this ideal, utility would enjoin, first, that laws and social arrangements should place the happiness or the interest of every individual as nearly as possible in harmony with the interest of the whole; and, secondly, that education and opinion, which have so vast a power over human character, should so use that power as to establish in the mind of every individual an indissoluble association between his own happiness and the good of the whole."

XXIII.

Private Pleasures and General Welfare.

In criticism of these indirect methods of establishing the identity of 'egoism' and 'altruism,' it may be said:

1. That the supposed relation between the private and the general happiness is extrinsic, and

hence always accidental and open to exception.

It is not contended that there is any order which *morally* demands that there be an identity of interests. It is simply argued that there are certain physical and psychological forces which operate, *as matter of fact*, to bring about such a result. Now we may admit, if we like, that such forces exist and that they are capable of accomplishing all that Bentham and Mill claim for them. But all that is established is, at most, a certain state of facts which is interesting as a state of facts, but which has no especial moral bearing. It is not pretended that there is in the very order of things any necessary and intrinsic connection between the happiness of one and of another. Such identity as exists, therefore, must be a mere external result of the action of certain forces. It is accidental. This being the case, how can it constitute the universal ideal of action? Why is it not open for an agent, under exceptional circumstances, to act for his own pleasure, to the exclusion of that of others? We may admit that, upon the whole (or that always, though this is wholly impossible to prove) in past experience, personal pleasure has been best attained by a certain regard for the pleasures of others; but the connection being wholly empirical (that is, of past instances and not of an intrinsic law), we may ask how it can be claimed that the same connection is *certain* to hold in this new case? Nor is it probable that any one would claim that the connection between individual pleasure and general pleasure had been so universal and invariable in past experience.

Intrinsic moral considerations (that is, those based on the very nature of human action) being put aside, a pretty strong case could be made out for the statement that individual happiness is best attained by ignoring the happiness of others. Probably the most that can be established on the other side is that a due prudence dictates that *some* attention be paid to the pleasures of others, in calculating one's own pleasures.

And this suggests:

2. That the end is still private pleasure, general pleasure being simply a means. Granting all that the hedonists urge, what their arguments prove is not that the general pleasure is the end of action, but that, private pleasure being the end, regard for the pleasures of others is one of the most efficient means of reaching it. If private pleasure is a selfish end, the end is not less selfish because the road to it happens to bring pleasure to others also.

See Royce, Religious Aspect of Philosophy, pp. 61–74.

3. The use of education and law to bring about this identity, presupposes that we already have the

ideal of the identity as something desirable to realize—it takes for granted the very thing to be proved. Why should it occur to men to use the private influence of opinion and education, and the public influences of law and penalty to identify private welfare with public, unless they were already convinced that general welfare was the end of conduct, the one desirable thing? What the hedonist has to do is to show how, from the end of private happiness, we may get to the end of general happiness. What Bentham and Mill do show is, that if we take general happiness as the end, we may and do use education and law to bring about an identity of personal and general pleasures. This may go undoubted, but the question how we get the general happiness as the end, the good, remains unanswered.

Nor is this all. The conception of general happiness, taken by itself, has all the abstractness, vagueness and uncertainty of that of personal happiness, multiplied indefinitely by the greater number of persons introduced. To calculate the effects of actions upon the general happiness—when happiness is interpreted as a state of feeling—is an impossibility. And thus it is that when one is speaking of pleasures one is really thinking of welfare, or well-being, or satisfied and progressive human lives. Happiness is considered as it would be, if determined by certain active and well defined interests, and thus the hedonistic theory, while contradicting itself, gets apparently all the support of an opposed theory. Universalistic hedonism thus, more or less expressly, takes for granted a social order, or community of persons, of which the agent is simply one member like any other. This is the ideal which it proposes to realize. In this way—although at the cost of logical suicide—the ideal gets a content and a definiteness upon which it is possible to base judgments.

That this social organization of persons is the ideal which Mill is actually thinking of, rather than any succession of states of agreeable sensation, is evident by his treatment of the whole subject. Mill is quite clear that education and opinion may produce *any* sort of feeling, as well as truly benevolent motives to actions. For example, in his critique of Whewell, he says, (Op. cit., p. 154): "All experience shows that the moral feelings are preëminently artificial, and the products of culture; that even when reasonable, they are no more spontaneous than the growth of corn and wine (which are quite as natural), and that the most senseless and pernicious feeling can as easily be raised to the utmost intensity by inculcation, as hemlock and thistles could be reared to luxuriant growth by sowing them instead of wheat." It is certainly implied here that legislation, education and public opinion must have as a presupposed standard the identity of general and private interests or else they may produce anything whatever. That is to say, Mill instead of arriving at his result of general happiness simply takes it for granted.

This fact and the further fact that he virtually defines happiness through certain objective interests and ends (thus reversing the true hedonistic position) is obvious from the following, (Mill, Op. cit., pp. 343–347): After again stating that the moral feelings are capable of cultivation in almost any direction, and stating that moral associations that are of artificial construction dissolve through the force of intellectual analysis (*cf.* his Autobiography, p. 136), and that the association of pleasure with the feeling of duty would similarly dissolve unless it had a *natural* basis of sentiment, he goes on. " But there is this basis of powerful *natural* sentiment. This firm foundation is that of the social feelings of mankind; the desire to be in unity with our fellow-creatures. *The social state is at once so natural, so necessary, and so habitual to man that except in some unusual circumstances, or by an effort of voluntary abstraction he never conceives of himself otherwise than as a member of a body.* Any condition, therefore, which is essential to a state of society becomes more and more an inseparable part of every person's conception of the state of things which he is born into, and which is the destiny of a human being." Mill then goes on to describe some of the ways in which the social unity manifests itself and influences the individual's conduct. Then the latter "comes, as though instinctively, to be conscious of himself as a being who *of course* pays regard to others. The good of others becomes to him a thing naturally and necessarily to be attended to, like any of the physical conditions of our existence. *The deeply-rooted conception which every individual even now has of himself as a social being tends to make him feel it as one of his natural wants, that there should be harmony between his feelings and aims and those of his fellow-*

creatures. This conviction is the ultimate sanction of the greatest happiness morality."

It is to be noticed that there is involved in this account three ideas, any one of which involves such a reconstruction of the pleasure theory as to be a surrender of hedonism.

1. There is, in one instance, a *natural* (or intrinsic) connection between the end of conduct and the feelings, and not simply an external or artificial bond. This is in the case of the social feelings. In other words, in one case the ideal, that is, happiness, is intrinsically, or necessarily connected with a certain kind of conduct, that flowing from the social impulses. This, of course, reverses hedonism for it makes happiness dependent upon a certain kind of conduct, instead of determining the nature of conduct according as it happens to result in pleasure or pain.

2. Man conceives of himself, of his end or of his destiny as a member of a social body, and this conception determines the nature of his wants and aims. That is to say, it is not mere happiness that a man wants, but a certain *kind* of happiness, that which would satisfy a man who conceived of himself as social, or having ends and interests in common with others.

3. Finally, it is not mere general "happiness" which is the end, at all. It is social unity; "har-

mony of feelings and aims," a beneficial condition for one's self in which the benefits of all are included. Instead of the essentially vague idea of states of pleasurable sensation we have the conception of a community of interests and ends, in securing which alone is true happiness to be found. This conception of the moral ideal we regard as essentially true, but it is not hedonism. It gives up wholly the notion that pleasure is the *desired*, and, since it sets up a standard by which it determines pleasure, it gives up equally the notion that pleasure as such is the *desirable.*

In addition to the works already referred to, the following will give fuller ideas of hedonism and utilitarianism: For historical treatment see Sidgwick, History of Ethics; Jodl, Geschichte der Ethik, Vol. II., pp. 432-468; Bain, Moral Science, Historical Mention; Guyau, La Morale Anglaise Contemporaine; Wallace, Epicureanism; Pater, Marius, the Epicurean. Paley, Moral and Political Philosophy; Grote, Examination of the Utilitarian Philosophy (especially fair and valuable criticism); Lecky, History of European Morals, Vol. I, ch. 1; Birks, Utilitarianism (hostile); Blackie, Four Phases of Morals: Essay on Utilitarianism (hostile); Gizycki, Students' Manual of Ethical Philosophy, (Coit's trans., favorable); Calderwood, Hand-Book of Moral Philosophy (opposed); Laurie, Ethica (*e. g.*, p. 10). "The object of will is not pleasure, not yet happiness, but reason-given law—the law of harmony; but this necessarily ascertained through feeling, and, therefore, through happiness."

Wilson and Fowler, Principles of Morals, Vol. I,

pp. 98-112; Vol. II, pp. 262-273. Paulsen, System der Ethik, pp. 195-210.

XXIV.

The Utilitarian Theory Combined With the Doctrine of Evolution. There has lately been an attempt to combine utilitarian morality with the theory of evolution. This position, chiefly as occupied by Herbert Spencer and Leslie Stephen, we shall now examine.

Alexander, also, Moral Order and Progress, makes large use of the theory of evolution, but does not attempt to unite it with any form of hedonism.

For the combination, at least three decided advantages are claimed over ordinary utilitarianism.

1. It transforms 'empirical rules' into 'rational laws.' The evolutionary hedonists regard pleasure as the good, but hold that the theory of evolution enables them to judge *of the relation of acts to pleasure* much better than the ordinary theory. As Mr. Spencer puts it, the ordinary theory is not scientific, because it does not fully recognize the principle of causation as existing between certain acts as causes, and pleasures (or pains) as effects. It undoubtedly recognizes that some acts *do* result in pain or pleasure, but does not show *how* or *why* they so result. By the aid of the theory of evolution we can demonstrate that certain acts *must* be beneficial because furthering evolution, and others painful because retarding it.

Spencer, Data of Ethics, pp. 5758. "Morality properly so-called—the science of right conduct—has for its object to determine *how* and *why* certain rules of conduct are detrimental, and certain other rules beneficial. Those good and bad results cannot be accidental, but must be necessary consequences of the constitution of things; and I conceive it to be the business of moral science to *deduce, from the laws of life and the conditions of existence,* what kinds of action *necessarily* tend to produce happiness, and what kinds to produce unhappiness. Having done this, its deductions are to be recognized as laws of conduct; and are to be conformed to irrespective of a direct estimation of happiness or misery. . . . . The objection which I have to the current utilitarianism is, that it recognizes no more developed form of utility —does not see that it has reached but the initial stage of moral science. . . . . It is supposed that in future, as now, utility is to be determined only by observation of results; and that there is no possibility of knowing by deduction from fundamental principles what conduct *must* be detrimental and what conduct *must* be beneficial." *Cf.* also ch. IX, and Stephen, Science of Ehtics, ch. IX.

It is contended, then, that by the use of the evolutionary theory, we may substitute certain conditions, which in the very nature of things tend to produce happiness, for a calculation, based upon observation of more or less varying cases in the past, of the probable results of the specific action. Thus we get a fixed objective standard and do away with all the objections based upon the uncertainty, vagueness and liability to exceptions, of the ordinary utilitarian morality.

Spencer, Op. cit., p. 162: "When alleging that empirical utilitarianism is but introductory to rational utilitarianism I pointed out that the last does not take welfare for its *immediate* object of pursuit, but takes for its immediate object of pursuit conformity to certain principles which, in the nature of things, causally determine welfare."

2. It reconciles 'intuitionalism' with 'empiricism.' The theory of evolution not only gives us an objective standard on which happiness necessarily depends, and from which we may derive our laws of conduct, instead of deriving them from observation of particular cases, but it enables us to recognize that there are certain moral ideas now innate or intuitive. The whole human race, the whole animal race, has for an indefinite time been undergoing experiences of what leads to pleasure and of what leads to pain, until finally the results of these experiences have become organized into our very physical and mental make-up. The first point was that we could substitute for consideration of results consideration of the causes which determine these results; the present point is that so far as we have to use results, we can use those of the race, instead of the short span of the individual's life.

Spencer, Op. cit., pp. 123-124. "The experiences of utility organized and consolidated through all past generations of the human race have been producing corresponding nervous modifications, which, by continued transmission and accumulation, have become in us certain faculties of moral intuition—certain emotions corresponding to right and wrong conduct, which have no apparent basis in the individual experiences of utility. . . . . The evolution hypothesis thus enables us to reconcile opposed moral theories. . . . . The doctrine of innate powers of moral perception become congruous with the utilitarian doctrine, when it is seen that preferences and aversions are rendered organic by inheritance of the effects of pleasurable and painful experiences in progenitors."

3. It reconciles 'egoism' with 'altruism.' As we have seen, the relation of personal pleasure to general happiness presents very serious difficulties to hedonism. It is claimed, however, that the very process of evolution necessitates a certain identity. The being which survives must be the being which has properly adapted himself to his environment, which is largely social, and there is assurance that the conduct will be adapted to the environment just in the degree in which pleasure is taken in acts which concern the welfare of others. If an agent has no pleasure in such acts he will either not perform them, or perform them only occasionally, and thus will not meet the conditions of surviving. If surrounding conditions demand constantly certain actions, those actions in time must come to be pleasurable. The conditions of survival demand altruistic action, and hence such action must become pleasurable to the agent (and in that sense egotistic).

"From the laws of life (Spencer Op. cit., p. 205) it must be concluded that unceasing social discipline will so mould human action, that eventually sympathetic pleasures will be pursued to the fullest extent advantageous to each and all. . . . . Though pleasure may be gained by giving pleasure, yet the thought of the sympathetic pleasure to be gained will not occupy consciousness, but only the thought of the pleasure given."

XXV.

Criticism of Evolutionary Utilitarianism.

Regarding the whole foregoing scheme, it may be said so far as it is true, or suggestive of truth, it is not hedonistic. It does not judge actions from their effects in the way of pleasure or pain, but it judges pleasures from the basis of an independent standard 'in the nature of things.' It is expressly declared that happiness is not to be so much the end, as the *test* of conduct, and it is not happiness in general, of every sort and kind, but a certain kind of happiness, happiness conditioned by certain modes of activity, that is the test. Spencer's hedonism in its final result hardly comes to more than saying that in the case of a perfect individual in a perfect society, every action whatever would be accompanied by pleasure, and that, therefore, *in such a society*, pleasure would be an infallible sign and test of the morality of action—a position which is not denied by any ethical writer whatever, unless a few extreme ascetics. Such a position simply determines the value of pleasure by an independent criterion, and then goes on to say *of pleasure so determined*, that it is the test of the morality of action. This may be true, but, true or not, it is not hedonistic.

Furthermore, this standard by which the nature of pleasure is determined is itself an ethical (that is, active) standard. We have already seen that Spencer conceives that the modes of producing happiness are to be deduced from the "laws of life and the conditions of existence". This might be, of course, a deduction from *physical* laws and conditions. But when we find that the laws and conditions which Spencer employs are mainly those of *social* life, it is difficult to see why he is not employing a strictly ethical standard. To deduce not right actions directly from happiness, but the kinds of actions which will produce happiness from a consideration of a certain ideal of social relationships seems like a reversal of hedonism; but this is what Mr. Spencer does.

XXVI.

The Real Criterion of Evolutionary Ethics.

Mr. Spencer expressly recognizes that there exists (1) an ideal code of conduct, formulating the conduct of the completely adapted man in the completely evolved society. Such a code is called absolute ethics as distinguished from relative ethics—a code the injunctions of which are alone to be considered "as absolutely right, in contrast with those that are relatively right or least wrong, and which, as a system of ideal conduct, is to serve as a standard for our guidance in solving, as well as we can, the problems of real conduct" (p. 275 of the Data of Ethics). The ideal code deals, it will be observed, with the behavior of the completely adapted man in a completely evolved society." This ideal as elsewhere stated, is "an ideal social being so constituted that his spontaneous activities are congruous with the conditions imposed by the social environment formed by other such beings. . . . . The ultimate man is one in whom there is a correspondence between all the promptings of his nature and all the requirements of his life as carried on in society" (p. 275). Furthermore, "to make the ideal man serve as a standard, he has to be defined *in terms of the conditions which his nature fulfill*—in terms of the objective requisites which must be met before conduct can be right" (p. 179). "Hence it is manifest that we must consider the ideal man as existing in the ideal social state" (p. 280).

Here we have in the most express terms the recognition of a final and permanent standard with reference to which the nature of happiness is determined, and the standard is one of social relationships. To be sure it is claimed that the standard is one which results in greatest happiness, but every ethical theory has always claimed that the ideal moral condition would be accompanied by the maximum possible happiness.

2. The ideal state is defined with reference to the end of evolution. That is, Spencer defines pleasure from an independent standard instead of using pleasure as the standard. This standard is to be got at by considering that idea of "fully evolved conduct" given by the theory of evolution. This fully evolved conduct implies: (i.) Greatest possible quantity of life, both in length and breadth; (ii.) Similar maintenance of life in progeny; and (iii.) Life in which there is no interference of actions by one with those of another, and, indeed, life in which the "members of a society give material help in the achievement of ends, thus rendering the "lives of all more complete". (See Chap. II of Data of Ethics). Furthermore, the "complete life here identified with the ideally moral life" may be otherwise defined as a life of perfect equilibrium (p. 74), or balance of functions (p. 90), and this considered not simply with reference to the individual, but also with reference to the relation of the individual to society. "Complete life in a complete society is but another name for complete equilibrium between the co-ordinated

activities of each social unit and those of the aggregate of units" (p. 74, and the whole of chap. V. See also pp. 169–170 for the position that the end is a society in which each individual has full functions freely exercised in due harmony, and is, p. 100, "the spontaneous exercise of duly proportioned faculties").

3. Not only is pleasure thus determined by an objective standard of "complete living in a complete society" but it is expressly recognized that *as things are now, pleasure is not a perfect guide to, or even test of action.* And this difficulty is thought to be removed by reference to the ideal state in which right action and happiness will fully coincide.

The failure of pleasure as a perfect test and guide of right conduct, comes out in at least three cases:—

1. There is the conflict of one set of pleasures with another, or of present happiness with future, one lot having to be surrendered for the sake of another. This is wrong, since pleasure as such is good, and, although a fact at present, exists only on account of the incomplete development of society. When there is "complete adjustment of humanity to the social state there will be recognition of the truth that actions are completely right only when, besides being conducive to future happiness, special

and general, they are immediately pleasurable, and that painfulness, not only ultimate but proximate, is the concomitant of actions which are wrong" (p. 29. See for various cases in which "pleasures are not connected with actions which must be performed" and for the statement that this difficulty will be removed in an ideal state of society, p. 77; pp. 85–87; pp. 98–99).

2. There is also, at present, a conflict of individual happiness with social welfare. In the first place, as long as there exist antagonistic societies, the individual is called upon to sacrifice his own happiness to that of others, but "such moralities are, by their definition, shown to belong to incomplete conduct; not to conduct that is fully evolved" (See pp. 133–137). Furthermore, there will be conflict of claims, and consequent compromises between one's own pleasure and that of others (p. 148), until there is a society in which there is "complete living through voluntary cooperation", this implying negatively that one shall not interfere with another and shall fulfill contracts, and positively that men shall spontaneously help to aid one another lives beyond any specified agreement (pp. 146–149).

3. There is, at present, a conflict of obligation with pleasure. Needed activities, in other words, have often to be performed under a pressure, which

either lessens the pleasure of the action, or brings pain, the act being performed, however, to avoid a greater pain (so that this point really comes under the first head). But "the remoulding of human nature into fitness for the requirements of social life, must eventually make all needful activities pleasurable, while it makes displeasurable all activities at variance with these requirements" (p. 183). "The things now done with dislike, through sense of obligation, will be done then with immediate liking" (p. 84, and p. 186; and pp. 255–256). All the quotations on these various points are simply so many recognitions that pleasure and pain as such are not tests of morality, but that they become so when morality is independently realized. Pleasure is *not* now a test of conduct, but becomes such a test as fast as activity becomes full and complete! What is this but to admit (what was claimed in Sec. XIII) that activity itself is what man wants; not *mere* activity, but the activity which belongs to man as man, and which therefore has for its realized content all man's practical relationships.

Of Spencer's conception of the ideal as something not now realized, but to be some time or other realized once for all, we have said nothing. But see below, Sec. 64, and also Alexander, Op. cit., pp. 264-277, and also James, Unitarian Review, Vol. XXII., pp. 212-213.

We have attempted, above, to deal with evolutionary ethics only in the one point of its supposed connection with pleasure as a standard. Accounts and criticisms of a broader scope will be found in Darwin, Descent of Man; Martineau, Op. cit., Vol. II, pp. 335–393; Schurman, Ethical Import of Darwinism; Sorley, Ethics of Naturalism, chapters V, and VI; Stephen, Science of Ethics, particularly pp. 31–34; 78-89; 359–379; Royce, Religious Aspect of Philosophy, pp. 74–85; Everett, Poetry, Comedy and Duty, Essay on the New Ethics; Seth in Mind, Jan. 1889, on Evolution of Morality; Dewey, Andover Review, Vol. VII, p. 570; Hyslop, Ibid., Vol. IX, p. 348.

XXVII.

Formal Ethics. We come now to the ethical theories which attempt to find the good not only in the will itself, but in the will irrespective of any end to be reached by the will. The typical instance of such theories is the Kantian, and we shall, therefore, make that the basis of our examination. Kant's theory, however, is primarily a theory not of the good, but of the nature of duty, and that makes a statement of his doctrine somewhat more difficult.

"The concept of good and evil must not be determined before the moral law (of which it seems as if it must be the foundation), but only after it and by means of it" (Abbott's Trans., p. 154).

Separating, as far as we can, his theory of the good from that of duty, we get the following results:

1. Goodness belongs to the will, and to that alone.

"Nothing can possibly be conceived, in the world or out of it, which can be called good without qualification except a good will." The will is not good because of what it brings about, or what it is fitted to bring about; that is, it is not good on account of its adaptation to any end outside of itself. It is good in itself. "It is like a jewel which shines by its own light, having its whole value in itself."

2. The good, then, is not to be found in any *object* of will or of desire, nor in the will *so far as it is directed towards an end outside itself.* For the will to be moved by inclination or by desire is for it to be moved for the sake of some external end, which, moreover, is always pleasure (Kant, *i. e.*, agrees with the hedonists regarding the object of desire, but on that very ground denies that pleasure is the good or the desirable). If, then, no object of desire can be the motive of a good will, what is its motive? Evidently only some principle derived from the will itself. The good will is the will which acts from regard to its own law.

3. What is the nature of this law? All objects of desire (*i. e.*, all material) have been excluded from it. It must, therefore, be purely formal. The only content of the law of the good will is the *idea of law itself.* The good will acts from reverences for law *as law.* It not only acts *in confor-*

mity with law, but has the conception of law as its directing spring.

4. There must, however, be some application of this motive of law in general to particular motives or acts. This is secured as follows: The idea of law carries with it the idea of universality or self-identity. To act from the idea of law is then so to act that the motive of action can be generalized—made a motive for all conduct. The good will is the *legislative* will; the will whose motive can be made a law for conduct universally. The question in a specific case is then: Can your motive here be made universal, *i. e.*, a law? If the action is bad, determined by an object of desire, it will be contingent and variable, since pleasures are different to different persons and to the same person from moment to moment. The will is good, then, when its motive (or maxim) is to be found solely in the *legislative form* of the action, or in its fitness to be generalized into a universal principle of conduct, and the law of the good will is: "Act so that the maxim of thy will can always at the same time hold good as a principle of universal legislation" (Abbott's Trans., p. 119; also p. 55).

5. The application may be illustrated by the following cases:

(*a*) Some one, wearied by what he conceives to be the entire misery of life proposes to commit suicide, but he asks himself whether this maxim based on the principle of self-love could become a universal law of nature; and "we see at once that a system of nature in which the very feeling, whose office is to compel men to the preservation of life, should lead men by a universal law to death, cannot be conceived without contradiction". That is to say, the principle of the motive which would lead a man to suicide cannot be generalized without becoming contradictory—it cannot be made a law universal.

(*b*) An individual wishes to borrow money which he knows that he cannot repay. Can the maxim of this act be universalized? Evidently not: "a system of nature in which it should be a universal law to promise without performing, for the sake of private good, would contradict itself, for then no one would believe the promise—the promise itself would become impossible as well as the end it had in view."

(*c*) A man finds that he has certain powers, but is disinclined to develop them. Can he make the maxim of such conduct a universal law? He cannot *will* that it should become universal. "As a rational being, he must will that his faculties be developed."

(*d*) A prosperous individual is disinclined to relieve the misery of others. Can his maxim be generalized? "It is impossible to *will* that such a principle should have the universal validity of a law of nature. For a will which resolved this would contradict itself, in as much as many cases might occur in which one would have need of the love and sympathy of others, and in which, by such a law of nature, sprung from his own will, he would deprive himself of all hope of the aid he desires."

In conclusion, then, the good is the good will itself, and the will is good in virtue of the bare form of its action, independently of all special material willed.

See Abbott's trans., pp. 9–46, 105–120. Caird's Critical Philosophy of Kant, Vol. II, pp. 171–181; 209–212.

XXVIII.

Relation of this Theory to Hedonism. The Kantian theory, as already noticed, agrees in its psychology with hedonism. It holds that pleasures are the objects of desire. But it reverses the conclusion which hedonism draws from this fact *as to the desirable.* Since pleasures are the object of desire, and pleasures can give no law, no universality to action, the end of action must be found wholly *outside* the pleasures, and wholly outside the desires. It can be found only in the bare law of the will itself.

1. Hedonism finds the end of conduct, or the desirable, wholly determined by the various particular desires which a man happens to have; Kant-

ianism holds that to discover the end of conduct, we must wholly exclude the desires.

2. Hedonism holds that the rightness of conduct is determined wholly by its consequences; Kantianism holds that the consequences have nothing to do with the rightness of an act, but that it is decided wholly by the motive of the act.

From this contrast, we may anticipate both our criticism of the Kantian theory and our conception of the true end of action. The fundamental error of hedonism and Kantianism is the same —the supposition that desires are for pleasure only. Let it be recognized that desires are for objects conceived as satisfying or developing the self, and that pleasure is incidental to this fulfillment of the capacities of self, and we have the means of escaping the one-sidedness of Kantianism of well as of hedonism. We can see that the end is neither the procuring of particular pleasures through the various desires, nor action from the mere idea of abstract law in general, but that it is the *satisfaction of desires according to law.* The desire in its particular character does not give the law; this, as we saw in our criticism of hedonism, is to take away all law from conduct and to leave us at the mercy of our chance desires as they come and go. On the other hand the law is not something wholly apart from the desires. This, as we shall see, is equally to deprive us of a law capable of governing conduct. The law is the law of the desires themselves—the harmony and adjustment of desires necessary to make them instruments in fulfilling the special destiny or business of the agent.

From the same point of view we can see that the criterion is found neither in the consequences of our acts *as pleasures*, nor *apart from consequences.* It is found indeed in the consequences of acts, *but in their complete consequences*:—those upon the agent and society, as helping or hindering them in fulfillment of their respective functions.

XXIX.

Criticism of Kantian Criterion of Conduct.

1. *With reference to the unification of the conduct of the individual.* Of pleasure as the object of desire, we need now say nothing further, but may proceed at once to the criticism of the theory that the will, acting according to the mere idea of law in general, is the end of man and hence that it is the criterion of the rightness or wrongness of his acts. We shall attempt to show that such an end is wholly empty, and that it fails (as much as hedonism) to unify conduct or to place any specific act as to its morality.

The difficulty of the end proposed by Kant is that it is an abstraction; that it is remote. The hedonist leaves out one element from conduct, and takes into account the merely particular or individualistic side; the Kantian abstracts the opposite element — the merely universal. The formal universal, or universal stripped of all particular content, has, considered as an end of action, at least three defects.

I. It is an end which would make impossible that very conduct of which it is taken to be the end—that is, moral conduct. In denying that pleasure is the end of action, we took pains to show that it (or rather the feeling due to the tension between pleasure of a state considered better and the pain of the experienced worse state) is a necessary element in the force impelling to action. The mere conception of an end is purely intellectual; there is nothing in it to move to action. It must be *felt* as valuable, as worth having, and as more valuable than the present condition before it can induce to action. It must *interest*, in a word, and thus excite desire. But if feeling is, as Kant declares, to be excluded from the motive to action, because it is pathological or related to pleasure as the object of desire, how can there be any force moving to action? The mind seems to be set over against a purely theoretical idea of an end, with nothing to connect the mind with the end. Unless the end interests, unless it arouses emotion, why should the agent ever aim at it? And if the law does excite feeling or desire, must not this, on Kant's theory, be desire for pleasure and thus vitiate the morality of the act? We seem to be in a dilemma, one side of which makes moral action impossible by taking away all inducing force, while the other makes it impossible by introducing an immoral factor into the motive.

Kant attempts to escape from this difficulty by claiming that there is one feeling which is rational, and not sensuous in quality, being excited not by the conception of pleasure or pain, but by that of the moral law itself. This is the feeling of reverence, and through this feeling we can be moved to moral action. Waiving the question whether the mere idea of law in general would be capable of arousing any moral sentiment—or, putting the matter from the other side, whether Kant gives us a true account of the feeling of reverence—it is clear that this admission is fatal to Kant's theory. If desire or feeling as such is sensuous (or *pathological*, as Kant terms it), what right have we to make this one exception? And if we can make this one exception, why not others? If it is possible in the case of reverence, why not in the case, say, of patriotism, or of friendship, or of philanthropy, or of love—or even of curiosity, or of indignation, or of desire for approbation? Kant's separation of reverence, as the one moral sentiment from all others as pathological, is wholly arbitrary. The only distinction we can draw is of the feelings as they well up naturally in reaction upon stimuli, sentiments not conceived and thus neither moral nor immoral, and sentiments as transformed by ends of action, in which case all without exception may be moral or immoral, according to the character of the end. The Kantian separation is not only arbitrary psychologically, but is false historically. So far is it from true that the only moral sentiment is reverence for law, that men must have been moved toward action for centuries by motives of love and hate and social regard, before they became capable of such an abstract feeling as reverence. And it may be questioned whether this feeling, as Kant treats it, is even the highest or ultimate form of moral sentiment—whether it is not transitional to love, in which there is complete union of the individual interest on one hand, and the objective end on the other.

For these criticisms at greater length, see Caird, Critical Philosophy of Kant, Vol. II, Bk. II, ch. IV.

II. The Kantian end would not bring about any system in conduct—on the contrary, it would tend to differences and collisions. What is required to give unity to the sphere of conduct is, as we have seen, a principle which shall comprehend all the motives to action, giving each its due place in contributing to the whole—a universal which shall organize the various particular acts into a harmonious system. Now Kant's conception of the good does not lead to such result. We may even say that it makes it impossible. According to Kant each act must be considered independently of every other, and must be capable of generalization on its own account. Each motive of action must be capable of being *itself* a universal law of nature. Each particular rule of action is thus made absolute, and we are left not with one universal which comprehends all particulars in their relations to one another, but literally with a lot of universals. These not only fail to have a unity, but each, as absolute, must contradict some other. If the principles always to tell the truth and always to preserve life are universal *in themselves*, and not universal simply *through their relation to some total and controlling principle of life*, it must be impossible to reconcile them when they come into conflict.

See Caird, Op. cit., Vol. II, pp. 187-190, and p. 215. *Cf.* "Treated as universal and without exception, even two such commands as *e. g.*, 'Thou shalt not steal,' and 'Thou shalt not kill,' must ultimately come into conflict with each other; for, if all other interests are to be postponed to the maintenance of the rights of property, it is impossible that all other interests should also be postponed to the preservation of human life—and to make either property or life an absolute end is to raise a particular into a universal, to treat a part as if it were a whole. But the true moral vindication of each particular interest cannot be found in elevating it into something universal and absolute, but only in determining its place in relation to the others in a complete system of morality."

III. The principle is so empty of all content that it does not enable us to judge of any specific act.

A caution should be noticed here, which is equally applicable to the criticism of hedonism: When it is said that the end does not enable us to judge of specific acts, the objection is not that the *theory* (Kantianism or hedonism, as the case may be) does not give us rules for moral conduct. It is not the business of any theory, however correct as a theory, to lay down rules for conduct. The theory has simply to discover what the *end* is, and it is the end in view which determines specific acts. It is no more the business of ethics to tell what in particular a man ought to do, than it is of trigonometry to survey land. But trigonometry must state the principles by which land *is* surveyed, and so ethics must state the end by which conduct *is* governed. The objection to hedonism and Kantianism is that the end they give does not *itself* stand in any practical relation to conduct. We do not object to Kantianism because the *theory* does not help us as to specific acts, but because the *end*, formal law, does not help us, while the real moral end must determine the whole of conduct.

Suppose a man thrown into the complex surroundings of life with an intelligence fully developed, but with no previous knowledge of right or wrong, or of the prevailing moral code. He is to know, however, that goodness is to be found in the good will, and that the good will is the will moved by the mere idea of the universality of law. Can we imagine such an one deriving from his knowledge any idea of what concrete ends he ought to pursue and what to avoid? He is surrounded by special circumstances calling for special acts, and all he knows is that *whatever* he does is to be done from respect for its universal or legislative quality. What community is there between this principle and *what* he is to do? There is no bridge from the mere thought of universal law to any concrete end coming under the law. There is no common principle out of which grows the conception of law on one hand, and of the various special ends of action, on the other.

Suppose, however, that ends are independently suggested or proposed, will the Kantian conception serve to *test* their moral fitness? Will the conception that the end must be capable of being generalized tell us whether this or that end is one to be followed? The fact is, that there is no end whatever that *in or by itself*, cannot be considered as self-identical, or as universal. If we presuppose a certain rule, or if we presuppose a certain moral order, it may be true that a given motive cannot be universalized without coming into conflict with this presupposed rule or order. But aside from some moral system into connection with which a proposed end may be brought, for purposes of comparison, lying is just as capable as truth-telling of generalization. There is no more contradiction in the motive of universal stealing than there is in that of universal honesty—unless there is as standard some order or system of things into which the proposed action is to fit as a member. And this makes not the bare universality of the act, but the system, the real criterion for determining the morality of the act.

Thus Mill remarks, regarding Kant's four illustrations (*Ante*, p. 80), that Kant really has to employ utilitarian considerations to decide whether the act is moral or not.

For the foregoing criticisms, see Bradley, Ethical Studies, Essay IV; Caird, Op. cit., Vol. II, pp. 185–186, and 212–214, and, indeed, the whole of ch. II of Bk. II.

XXX.

Criticism of Kantian Criterion of Conduct.

2. *With reference to the furnishing of a common good or end.* If the Kantian end is so formal and empty as not to enable us to bring into relation with one another the various acts of one individual, we may agree, without argument, that it does not provide us with an end which shall unify the acts of different men into a connected order of conduct. The moral end, the acting from regard

for law as law, is presented to each individual by himself, entirely apart from his relations to others. That he has such relations may, indeed, furnish additional material to which the law must be applied, but is something to which the character of the law is wholly indifferent. The end is not in itself a social end, and it is a mere accident if in any case social considerations have to be taken into account. It is of the very quality of the end that it appeals to the individual as an isolated individual.

It is interesting to note the way in which Kant, without expresslly giving up the purely formal character of the moral end, gives it more and more content, and that content social. The moral law is not imposed by any external authority, but by the rational will itself. To be conscious of a universal self-imposed law is to be conscious of one's self as having a universal aspect. The source of the law and its end are both in the will—in the rational self. Thus man is an end to himself, for the rational self is man. Such a being is a person—"Rational beings are *persons*, because their nature marks them out as ends in themselves, *i. e.*, as beings who should never be used merely as means. . . . . Such beings are not ends simply *for us*, whose existence as brought about by our action has value, but *objective ends*, *i. e.*, beings whose existence is an end in itself, an end for which no other end can be substituted so as to reduce it to a mere means." Thus, we get a second formula. "Always treat humanity, both in your own person and in the person of others, as an end and never merely as a means." (Abbott's Trans., pp. 46–47; Caird, Op. cit., Vol. II, 219). Here the criterion of action is no longer the bare self-consistency of its motive, but its consistency with the rational nature of the agent, that which constitutes him a person. And, too, "the will of every rational being is likewise a universally law-giving will." (Abbott, p. 49). The conception of humanity embodied in others as well as in one's self is introduced, and thus our criterion is socialized. Even now, however, we have a lot of persons, each of whom has to be considered as an end in himself, rather than a social unity as to which every individual has an equal and common reference. Kant advances to this latter idea in his notion of a "Kingdom of ends." "We get the idea of a complete and systematically connected totality of all ends—a whole system of rational beings as ends in themselves as well as of the special ends which each of them may set up for himself—*i. e.*, a kingdom of ends. . . . . Morality is the reference of all deeds to the legislation which alone can make such a kingdom possible." (See Abbott's Trans., pp. 51-52). This transformation of a mere formal universal into a society or kingdom of persons—while not sufficiently analyzed as Kant states it (see Caird, Vol. II, pp. 225-226)—gives us truly a social criterion, and we shall hereafter meet something resembling it as the true ideal. As finally stated, it does not differ in essential content from Mill's individual who "conceives of himself only as a member of a body," or from Spencer's free man in a free society.

XXXI.

Value of Kantian Theory. We must not leave the Kantian theory with the impression that it is simply the caprice of a philosopher's brain. In two respects, at least, it presents us, as we shall see, with elements that must be adopted; and even where false it is highly instructive.

Kant's fundamental error is in his conception that all desires or inclinations are for private pleasure, and are, therefore, to be excluded from the conception of the moral end. Kant's conclusion, accordingly, that the good will is purely formal follows inevitably if ever it is granted that there is any intrinsic opposition between inclination as such, and reason or moral law as such. If there is such an opposition, *all* desire must be excluded from relation to the end. We cannot make a compromise by distinguishing between higher and lower desires. On the contrary, if the end is to have content, it must include all desires, leaving out none as in itself base or unworthy. Kant's great negative service was showing that the ascetic principle logically results in pure formalism—meaning by ascetic principle that which disconnects inclinations from moral action.

Kant's positive service was, first, his clear insight into the fact that the good is to be found only in activity; that the will itself, and nothing beyond itself, is the end; and that to adopt any other doctrine, is to adopt an immoral principle, since it is to subordinate the will (character, self and personality), to some outside end. His second great service was in showing the necessity of putting in abeyance the immediate satisfaction of each desire as it happens to arise, and of subordinating it to some law not to be found in the particular desire. He showed that not the particular desire, but only the desire as controlled by the idea of law could be the motive of moral action. And if he fell into the error of holding that this meant that the desire must be excluded from the moral motive, this error does not make it less true that every particular desire must be controlled by a universal law. The truth of asceticism is that the desire must be checked until subordinated to the activity of the whole man. See Caird, Op. cit., Vol. II, p. 200; pp. 203–207; 226–227.

XXXII.

The Problem and Its Solution. If we gather together the results of our observations of hedonism and of Kantianism we get something like the following problem and solution in outline. The end of action, or the good, is the realized will, the developed or satisfied self. This satisfied self is found neither in the getting of a lot of pleasures through the satisfaction of desires just as they happen to arise, nor in obedience to law simply because it is law. It is found in *satisfaction of desires according to law.* This law, however, is not something external to the desires, but is their own law. Each desire is only one striving of character for larger action, and the only way in which it can really find satisfaction (that is, pass from inward striving into outward action) is *as* a manifestation of character. A desire, taken as a desire for its own apparent or direct end *only*, is an abstraction. It is a desire for an entire and continuous activity, and its satisfaction requires that it fitted into this entire and continuous activity; that it be made conformable to the conditions which will bring the whole man into action. It is this fitting-in which is the law of the desire—the 'universal' controlling its particular nature. This 'fitting-in' is no mechanical shearing off, nor stretching out, but a reconstruction of the natural desire till it becomes an expression of the whole man. The problem then is to find that special form of character, of self, which includes and transforms all special desires. This form of character is at once the Good and the Law of man.

We cannot be content with the notion that the end is the satisfaction of the self, a satisfaction at once including and subordinating the ends of the particular desire. This tells us nothing positive—however valuable it may be negatively in warning us against one-sided notions—until we know *what* that whole self is, and *in what* concretely its satisfaction consists. As the first step towards such a more concrete formula, we may say:

XXXIII.

The Moral End or the Good is the Realization by a Person and as a Person of Individuality.

In saying that this realization is *by a person* and *as a person* we are saying nothing new. We are simply repeating what we have already learned about moral conduct (Sec. III). Conduct is not that which simply reaches certain consequences—a bullet shot from a rifle does that; there is conduct only when the consequences are foreseen; made the reason of action. A person is a being capable of conduct—a being capable of proposing to himself ends and of attempting to realize them.

But what is the meaning of the rest of the formula? What do we mean by individuality? We may distinguish two factors—or better two aspects, two sides—in individuality. On one side, it means special disposition, temperament, gifts, bent, or inclination; on the other side, it means special station, situation, limitations, surroundings, opportunities, etc. Or, let us say, it means *specific capacity* and *specific environment.* Each of these elements, apart from the other, is a bare abstraction and without reality. Nor is it strictly correct to say that individuality is constituted by these two factors *together.* It is rather, as intimated above, that each is individuality looked at from a certain point of view, from within or from without.

If we are apt to identify individuality with the inner side alone, with capacity apart from its surroundings, a little reflection will show the error. Even the most devoted adherent of "self-culture" would not hold that a gift could be developed, or a disposition manifested, in isolation from all exterior circumstances. Let the disposition, the gift be what it may (amiable or irascible, a talent for music or for abstract science, or for engineering), its existence, to say nothing of its culture, apart from some surroundings is bare nonsense. If a person shuts himself up in a closet or goes out into the desert the better to cultivate his capacities, there is still the desert or the closet there; and it is as conditioned by them, and with reference to them that he must cultivate himself. For more is true than that, as a matter of fact, no man can wholly withdraw himself from surroundings; the important point is that the manner and the purpose of exercising his capacity is always *relative* to and *dependent* upon the surroundings. Apart from the environment the capacity is mere emptiness; the exercise of capacity is always establishing a relation to something exterior to itself. All we can say of capacity apart from environment is that *if* certain circumstances were supplied, there would be something there. We call a capacity *capability*, possibility, as if for the very purpose of emphasizing the necessity of external supplementing.

We get the same fact, on the other side, by calling to mind that circumstances, environment are not indifferent or irrelevant to individuality. The difference between one individual and another lies as much in the station in which each is placed as in the capacity of each. That is to say, environment enters into individuality as a constituent factor, helping make it what it is.

On the other hand, it is capacity which makes the environment really an environment *to* the individual.

The environment is not simply the facts which happen objectively to lie about an agent; it is such part of the facts as may be *related* to the capacity and the disposition and gifts of the agent. Two members of the same family may have what, to the outward eye, are exactly the same surroundings, and yet each may draw from these surroundings wholly unlike stimulus, material and motives. Each has a different environment, made different by his own mode of selection; by the different way in which his interests and desires play upon the plastic material about him. It is not, then, the environment as physical of which we are speaking, but as it appeals to consciousness, as it is affected by the make-up of the agent. This is the *practical* or *moral* environment. The environment is not, then, what is then and there present in space. To the Christian martyr the sufferings of his master, and the rewards of faithfulness to come to himself were more real parts of his environment than the stake and fire. A Darwin or a Wallace may find his environment in South America or the Philippine Islands—or, indeed, in every fact of a certain sort wherever found upon the earth or in whatever geological era. A man of philanthropic instincts may find *his* environment among Indians or Congo negroes. Whatever, however near or remote in time and space, an individual's capacities and needs relate him to, is his environment. The moment we realize that only what one conceives as proper material for calling out and expressing some internal capacity is a part of his surroundings, we see not only that capacity depends upon environment, but that environment depends upon capacity. In other words, we see that each in itself is an abstraction, and that the real thing is the individual who is constituted by capacity and environment in their relation to one another.

Function is a term which we may use to express union of the two sides of individuality. The idea of function is that of an active relation established between power of doing, on one side, and something to be done on the other. To exercise a function as a student is not to cultivate tastes and possibilities internally; it is also to meet external demands, the demands of fact, of teachers, of others needing knowledge. The citizen exercises his function not simply in cultivating sentiments of patriotism within; one has to meet the needs of the city, the country in which one lives. The realization of an artistic function is not poring over emotions of beauty pumped up within one's self; it is the exercise of some calling. On the other hand, it hardly needs saying that the function of a student, a citizen, an artist, is not exercised in bare conformity to certain external requirements. Without the inner disposition and inclination, we call conduct dead, perfunctory, hypocritical. An activity is not functional, unless it is organic, expressing the life of the agent.

A function thus includes two sides—the external and the internal—and reduces them to elements in one activity. We get an analogy in any animal function. The digestive function includes the material appropriated, just as much as it does the organ appropriating. It is the service, the work which the organ does *in* appropriating material. So, morally, function is capacity *in action*; environment transformed into an element in personal service.

Thus we get another formula for the moral end:

The performance by a person of his specific function, this function consisting in an activity which realizes wants and powers with reference to their peculiar surroundings.

XXXIV.

Moral Functions as Interests.

If morality consists in the exercise of one's *specific* functions, it follows that no *detailed* account of the content of the moral end can possibly be given. This content is thoroughly individual or infinite. It is concrete to the core, including every detail of conduct, and this not in a rigid formula, but in the movement of life. All we can do is, by abstraction, to select some of the main features of the end, such as the more common and the more permanent. While each individual has his own particular functions, which can no more be exhausted by definition or description than the qualities of any other individual object, it is also true that we can recognize certain typical functions to be found permanently and in ali. These make, as it were, the skeleton of the moral end which each clothes with his own flesh and blood.

Functions are *interests*—objective interests were not the term tautological. Interests have three traits worth special mention.

1. They are *active.* An interest is not an emotion produced from without. It is the reaction of the emotion to the object. Interest is identified, in ordinary speech, with attention; we *take* an inter-

est, or, if we say simply 'interested,' that involves some excitation, some action just beginning. We talk of a man's interests, meaning his occupations or range of activities.

2. They are *objective.* The emotion aroused goes out to some object, and is fixed upon that; we are always interested *in something.* The active element of interest is precisely that which takes it out of the inner mood itself and gives it a terminus, an end in an object.

3. An interest is *satisfaction.* It is its own reward. It is not a striving for something unrealized, or a mere condition of tension. It is the satisfaction in some object which the mind already has. This object may be possessed in some greater or less degree, in full realization or in faint grasp, but interest attaches to it as possessed. This differentiates it from desire, even where otherwise the states are the same. Desire refers to the lack, to what is not present to the mind. One state of mind may be called both interest in, and desire for, knowledge, but desire emphasizes the unknown, while interest is on account of the finding of self, of intelligence, in the object. Interest is the union in feeling, through action, of self and an object. An interest in life is had when a man can practically identify himself with some object lying beyond his immediate or already acquired self

and thus be led to further expression of himself.

To have an interest, then, is to be alert, to have an object, and to find satisfaction in an activity which brings this object home to self.

Not every interest carries with it *complete* satisfaction. But no interest can be wholly thwarted. The purer the interest, the more the interest is in the object for its own sake, and not for that of some ulterior consequence, the more the interest fulfills itself. "It is better to have loved and lost than never to have loved at all", and love is simply the highest power of interest—interest freed from all extrinsic stuff.

Of the interests, two abstract forms may be recognized, interest in persons and interest in things. And these may be subdivided: Interest in persons: interest in *self* and *others*. Interest in things—into their contemplation (*knowledge*) and into their production (*art*). And art again may be either productive of things to be contemplated (fine art), or useful — manufactures, industry, etc. The moral end, then, or the Good will consist in the exercise of these interests, varied as they may be in each individual by the special turn which his capacities and opportunities take.

XXXV.

The Exercise of Interests as the Moral End. Let us now, as a means of rendering our conception of the moral end more concrete, consider briefly each of the forms of interest.

1. Interest in self. We must free ourselves from any notion that an interest in self is non-moral, if not actually immoral. The latter position is seldom consciously assumed, but it is not uncommon to have interest in self, under the name of prudence, marked off from the moral sphere. Interest in self, if the interest is pure, is just as much an interest in the moral end as interest in anything or anybody else. Interest in self may take the form of selfishness, or of sentimentalism; but this is only an *impure* interest, an interest not in self, but in some conseqences to which the self may be directed. Interest in self may take many forms, according to the side of self which is the object of attention, and according to the range of the self taken into account. A *rudimentary* form is prudence, but even this, instead of being non-moral, is, in proper place and degree, moral, as moral as benevolence; and, if not in its proper place, immoral. From such an interest there are all stages up to the interest in self as it most deeply and broadly is, the sense of honor, moral dignity, self-respect, conscientiousness, that attempt to be and to make the most of one's self, which is at the very root of moral endeavor.

The ground that is usually given for making the distinction between Prudence, Self-Regard, Self-Love as non-moral, and Benevolence, Altruism etc., as moral, is that in the former case a mere regard for one's own advantage dictates proper conduct, while in the latter case there must be a positive virtuous intent. We may, for example, be pointed to some cool calculating man who takes care of his health and his property, who indeed is generally 'prudent', because he sees that it is for his advantage, and be told that while such an end is not immoral it is certainly not moral. But in return it must be asked what is meant here by advantage? If by it is meant private pleasure, or advantage over somebody else, then this conduct does not spring from interest in self at all, but from interest in some exterior consequence, and as springing from such an impure interest is not simply non-moral, but positively immoral. On the other hand, if 'advantage' means regard for one's whole function, one's place in the moral order, then such interest in self is moral. Care for bodily health in the interest of efficiency in conduct is supremely moral beside reckless disregard of it in the interest of some supposed higher or more spiritual function.

If it is meant that conduct is immoral because it springs from some interest on the part of the agent, the reply is that all conduct must so arise, and that any other supposition leads us immediately into asceticism and into formalism.

2. Interest in others. The generic form of interest in others is sympathy, this being specified by the various forms of social organization of which the individual is a member. A person is, we have seen, one who can conceive of ends and can act to realize these ends. Only a person, therefore, can conceive of others as ends, and so have true sympathy.

It is not meant, of course, that animals do not perform acts which, *de facto*, are altruistic or even self-sacrificing. What is meant is that the animal does not act from the *idea* of others of his kind as ends in themselves. If the animal does so act, it cannot be denied the name of person.

True interest in others is pure, or disinterested, in the sense of having no reference to some further and external consequence to one's self. Interest in others need not be moral (or pure) any more than interest in self is necessarily immoral (or impure). It is a mistake to distinguish interest in self as *egoistic* and interest in others as *altruistic*. Genuine interests, whatever their object, are both egoistic and altruistic. They are egoistic simply because they *are interests*—imply satisfaction in a realized end. If man is truly a social being, constituted by his relationships to others, then social action must inevitably realize himself, and be, in that sense, egoistic. And on the other hand, if the individual's interest in himself is in himself *as* a member of society, then such interest is thoroughly altruistic. In fact, the very idea of altruism is likely to carry a false impression when it is so much insisted upon, as it is nowadays in popular literature, as the essence of morality. The term as used seems to imply that the mere giving up of one's self to others, as others, is somehow moral. Just as there may be an immoral interest in self, so there may be an immoral 'altruism.' It is immoral in any case to sacrifice the actual relationships in the case, those which demand action, to some feeling outside themselves—as immoral when the feeling to which the sacrifice is offered up is labelled 'benevolence', as when it is termed 'greediness'. It is no excuse when a man gives unwisely to a beggar that he feels benevolent. *Moral* benevolence is the feeling directed toward a certain end which is known to be the fit or right end, the end which expresses the situation. The question is as to the *aim* in giving. Apart from this aim, the act is simply relieving the agent's own feelings and has no moral quality. Rather it is immoral; for feelings do have a moral *capacity*, that is, a relation to ends of action, and hence to satisfy them on their account, to deprive them of their practical reference, is bad. Aside from what this illustrates, there is a tendency in the present emphasis of altruism to erect the principle of charity, in a sense which implies continued social inequality, and social slavery, or undue dependence of one upon another, into a fundamental moral principle. It is well to "do good" to others, but it is much better to do this by securing for them the freedom which makes it possible for them to get along in the future without such 'altruism' from others. There is what has been well termed an "egotism of renunciation"; a desire to do for others which, at bottom, is simply an attempt to regulate their conduct. Much of altruism is an egoism of a larger radius, and its tendency is to "manufacture a gigantic self", as in the case where a father sacrifices everything for his children or a wife for her husband.

See Caird, Op. cit., Vol. II, p. 402. See also Hinton, The Law Breaker, p. 287: "The real meaning of the difficulty about a word for "regard for others" is that we do not want it. It would mislead us if we had it. It is not a regard for *others* that we need, but simply a *true* regard, a regard to the facts, to nature; it is only a truth to facts in our regard, and its nature is obscured by a reference to "others", as if that were the essential point. . . . . It is not as being for others, but as being *true*, that the regard for others is demanded."

Some ethical writers have gone to the other extreme and held that all benevolence is a disguised or an enlightened selfishness, since having a necessary reference to self. The reference to self must be admitted; unless the action springs from an interest of the agent himself the act may be outwardly useful, but cannot be moral. But the argument alluded to inverts the true relation involved. If a man's interests are such that he can find satisfaction only in the satisfaction of others, what an absurdity to say that his acting from these interests is selfish! The very fact of such identity of self with others in his interest is the proof of his unselfishness.

See Leslie Stephen, Science of Ethics, p. 241, for an admirable discussion of this difficulty. When it is said that your pain is painful to me, he says, the inference is often "insinuated that I dislike your pain because it is painful to me in some special relation. I do not dislike it *as* your pain, but in virtue of some particular consequence. such, for example, as its making you less able to render me a service. In that case *I do not really object to your pain as your pain at all*, but only to some removable and accidental consequences." (And see his whole treatment of sympathy, pp. 230–245). The whole question is shown to come to this: Is my interest in, my sympathy with, your joy and sorrow as such, or in your joy and sorrow as contributing to mine? If the latter, of course the interest is selfish, not being an interest in others at all. But if the former, then the fact that such sympathy involves one's own satisfaction is the best proof that man is not selfishly constructed. When Stephen goes on to say that such sympathy does not involve the existence of a real unity larger than the individual, he seems to me to misread his own facts, probably because he conceives of this unity as some abstract or external thing.

Discussion regarding self-love and benevolence, or, in modern phrase, egoism and altruism, has been rife in English ethics since the time of Hobbes, and especially of Shaftesbury and Butler. See, in particular, the Sermons of the latter, which gave the central point of discussion for almost a century. With reference to the special weakness of this point of view, with its co-ordination of two independent principles. see Green, Philosophical Works, Vol. III, pp. 99–104. The essential lack (the lack which we have tried to make good in the definition of individuality as the union of capacity and surroundings in function), was the failure to analyze the idea of the individual. Individuality being defined as an exclusive principle, the inevitable result was either (i.) the "disguised selfishness" theory; or (ii.) the assumption of two fundamentally different principles in man. The ordinary distinction between prudence and virtue is an echo of the latter theory. Then, finally, (iii.) a third principle, generally called conscience by Butler, was brought in as umpire in the conflict of prudence and virtue.

Suggestive modern treatment of the matter, from a variety of points of view, will be found in Spencer, Data of Ethics, chs. XI–XIII; Stephen, Op. cit., ch. VI; Sidgwick, Op. cit., Bk. V, ch. VII; Royce, Op. cit., ch. IV; Sorley, Ethics of Naturalism, pp. 134–150; Alexander, Op. cit., pp. 172–180; Caird, Op. cit., Vol. II, pp. 400–405; Paulsen, System der Ethik, pp. 295–311.

3. Interest in Science and Art. Man is interested in the world about him; the knowledge of the nature and relations of this world become one of his most absorbing pursuits. Man identifies himself with the meaning of this world to the point that he can be satisfied only as he spells out and reads its meaning. (See, for example, Browning's "Grammarian's Funeral".) The scientific interest is no less a controlling motive of man than the personal interest. This knowledge is not a means for having agreeable sensations; it is not dilettanteism or 'love of culture"; it is interest in the large and goodly frame of things. And so it is with art; man has interests which can be satisfied only in the reconstruction of nature in the way of the useful and the beautiful.

I have made no distinction between 'fine' and 'useful' art. The discussion of this question does not belong here, but the rigid separation of them in æsthetic theory seems to me to have no justification. Both are products of intelligence in the service of interests, and the only difference is in the range of intelligence and interests concerned. 'Use' is a *limited* service and hence implies an external end; beauty is complete use or service, and hence not mere use at all, but self-expression. Historically, all art which has not been merely sentimental and 'literary' has sprung from interest in good workmanship in the realizing of an idea.

It seems as if here interests violated their general law, and, in the case of use at least, were an interest in some ulterior end. But it may be questioned whether a carpenter whose aim was consciously beyond the work he was doing, would be a good workman—and this whether the further end is his own private advantage, or social benefit at large. The thought of the further benefit to self and of the utility to accrue to some one else, will, if it becomes a *part* of what he is doing, undoubtedly intensify his interest—it must do so, for it enlarges its content. But to *identify* one's own or another's well-being with work, and to make the work a mere *means* to this welfare, are two quite different things. The good artisan "has his heart in his work". His self-respect makes it necessary for him to respect this technical or artistic capacity, and to do the best by it that he can without scrimping or lowering. To a good business man business is not the mere means to money-making; and it is sentimentalism (and hence immoral) to demand that it be a mere means to the good of society. The business, if it is a moral one (and *any* business, *so far* as it is thus carried on, is moral), is carried on for the sake of the activity itself, as a realizing of capacity in a specific situation.

XXXVI.

The Moral Quality of Science. We seem, however, to meet here, in relation to science and art, a difficulty which threatens our whole theory. Can it be claimed, it may be asked, that devotion to science or art constitutes goodness in the same sense that devotion to the interests of one's family or state constitutes it? No one doubts that a good father or a good citizen is a good man, in so far forth. Are we ready to say that a good chemist or good carpenter, or good musician is, in so far, a good man? In a word, is there not a reference to the good of persons present in one case and absent in another, and does not its absence preclude the scientific and artistic activities from any share, *as such*, in the moral end?

It must be remembered that the moral end does not refer to some consequence which happens, *de facto*, to be reached. It refers to an end *willed*; *i. e.*, to an idea held to and realized as an idea. And this fact shows us the way to meet the query, in part at least. If, when we say good carpenter, or good merchant, we are speaking from the standpoint of results, independently of the idea conceived as end in the mind of the agent; if we mean simply, 'we like what that man does', then the term good has no moral value. A man may paint 'good' pictures and not be, in so far, a good man, but in this sense a man may *do* a great deal of 'good', and yet not be a good man. It was agreed at the outset that moral goodness pertains to the kind of idea or end which a man clings to, and not to what he happens to effect visibly to others.

If a scientific man pursues truth as a mere means to reputation, to wealth, etc., we do not (or should not) hesitate to call him immoral.

This does not mean that if he *thinks* of the reputation, or of weath, he is immoral, for he may foresee wealth and the reputation as necessarily bound up in what he is doing; it may become a part of the end. It means that if knowledge of truth is a *mere means* to an end beyond it, the man is immoral.

What reason is there why we should not call him moral if he does his work for its own sake, from interest in this cause which takes him outside his "own miserable individuality", in Mill's phrase? After all, the phrase a 'good father' means but a character manifesting itself in certain relations, as is right according to these relations; the phrase has moral significance not in itself, but with reference to the end aimed at by character. And so it is with the phrase 'a good carpenter.' That also means devotion of character to certain outer relations for their own sake. These relations may not be so important, but that is not lack of moral meaning.

XXXVII.

Adjustment to Environment. So far we have been discussing the moral ideal in terms of its inner side — capacity, interest. We shall now discuss it on its outer or objective side—as 'adjustment to environment' in the phrase made familiar by the evolutionists. Certain cautions, however, must be noted in the use of the phrase. We must keep clearly in mind the relativity of environment to inner capacity; that it exists only as one element of function. Even a plant must do something more than adjust itself *to* a fixed environment; it must assert itself *against* its surroundings, subordinating them and transforming them into material and nutriment; and, on the surface of things, it is evident that *transformation* of existing circumstances is moral duty rather than mere reproduction of them. The environment must be plastic to the ends of the agent.

But admitting that environment is made what it is by the powers and aims of the agent, what sense shall we attribute to the term adjustment?

Not bare conformity to circumstances, nor bare external reproduction of them, even when circumstances are taken in their proper moral meaning. The child in the family who simply adjusts himself *to* his relationships in the family, may be living a moral life only in outward seeming. The citizen of the state may transgress no laws of the state, he may punctiliously fulfill every contract, and yet be a selfish man. True adjustment must consist in *willing* the maintenance and development of moral surroundings as *one's own end.* The child must take the spirit of the family into himself and live out this spirit according to his special membership in the family. So a soldier in the army, a friend in a mutual association, etc. Adjustment to intellectual environment is not mere conformity of ideas to facts. It is the living assimilation of these facts into one's own intellectual life, and maintaining and asserting them as *truth.*

There are environments existing prior to the activities of any individual agent; the family, for example, is prior to the moral activity of a child born into it, but the point is to see that 'adjustment', to have a moral sense, means *making the environment a reality for one's self.* A true description of the case would say that the child takes for his own end, ends already existing for the wills of others. And, in making them his own, he creates and supports for himself an environment that already exists for others. In such cases there is no special transformation of the existing environment; there is simply the process of making it the environment for one's self. So in learning, the child simply appropriates to himself the intellectual environment already in existence for others. But in the activity of the man of science there is more than such personal reproduction and creation; there is increase, or even reconstruction of the prior environment. While the ordinary citizen hardly does more than make his own the environment of ends and interests already sustained in the wills of others, the moral reformer may remake the whole. But whether one case or the other, adjustment is not outer conformity; it is living realization of certain relations in and through the will of the agent.

XXXVIII.

The Moral End is the Realization of a Community of Wills. Since the performance of function is, on the other side, the creation, perpetuation, and further development of an environment, of relations to the wills of others, its performance *is a common good.* It satisfies others who participate in the environment. The member of the family, of the state, etc., in exercising his function, contributes to the whole of which he is a member by realizing its spirit in himself. But the question discussed in section XXXVI recurs under another aspect. Granting that the satisfying of personal interests realizes a common good, what shall we say of the impersonal interests—interests in science and art. Is the good carpenter or chemist not only in so far a good man, but also a good social member? In other words, does every form of moral activity realize a common good, or is the moral end partly social, partly non-social?

One objection sometimes brought to the doctrine that the moral end is entirely social, may be now briefly dismissed. This is the objection that a man has moral duties toward *himself*. Certainly, but what of *himself*? If he is essentially a social member, his duties toward himself have a social basis and bearing. The only relevant question is whether one is wholly a social member—whether scientific and artistic activities may not be non-social.

The ground here taken is that the moral end is wholly social. This does not mean that science and art are means to some social welfare beyond themselves. We have already stated that even the production of utilities must, as moral, be its own end. The position then is that intellectual and artistic interests *are themselves* social, when considered in the completeness of their relations—that interest in the development of intelligence is, in and of itself, interest in the well-being of society.

Unless this be true there is no moral end at all,

but only moral ends. There is no comprehensive unity in life, but a number of ends which, being irreducible to a common principle, must be combined on the best principle of compromise available. We have no 'The Good', but an aggregate of fragmentary ends.

It helps nothing to say that this necessary unity is found in the *self* to be realized, unless we are pointed to something in the self that unites the social and non-social functions. Our objection is that the separation of intellectual interests from social makes a chasm in the self.

For the same reason it follows that in the case of a collision of social with intellectual ends—say the conflict of a man's interests as a member of a family with his interests in new scientific discovery—no reconciliation is possible. If the interests are forms of social interest, there is a common end in both, on the basis of which the conflict can be resolved. While such considerations do not prove that there is but one end, and that social, they may well make us hesitate about carelessly taking a position of which they are the logical consequence.

Of course, every one recognizes that a certain amount of scientific and artistic interest is social in character. A certain amount of interest in truth, or in intelligence, a certain amount of susceptibility to beauty, a certain amount of devotion to utility, are universally recognized to be necessary to make judicious, agreeable and efficient social members. The whole system of modern education has meaning only on this supposition.

More than this: A certain amount of intelligence, and a certain amount of susceptibility to embodied ideals, *must* exist to give moral conduct. A moral end is, as we have seen, always a *conception*, an idea. The very act of bringing conduct out of the impulsive into the moral sphere, depends upon the development of intelligence so as to transform a feeling into the perception of a situation. And, as we watch moral development from childhood to maturity, is it not evident that progress consists in power to conceive of larger and better defined ends? to analyze the situation which demands active response, the function which needs exercise, into specific relations, instead of taking it partially or even upon some one else's say so? Conduct, so far as not based upon an intelligent recognition and realization of the relationships involved, is either sentimental, or *merely* habitual—in the former case immoral, and in the latter failing of the complete morality possible.

If the necessary part played in conduct by artistic cultivation is not so plain, it is largely because 'Art' has been made such an unreal Fetich—a sort of superfine and extraneous polish to be acquired only by specially cultivated people. In reality, living is itself the supreme art; it requires fineness of touch; skill and thoroughness of workmanship; susceptible response and delicate adjustment to a situation apart from reflective analysis; instinctive perception of the proper harmonies of act and act, of man and man. Active art is the embodiment of ideals; the clothing of ideas otherwise abstract in their peculiar and fit garb of concrete outward detail; passive art is the quick and accurate response to such embodiments as are already made. What were human conduct without the one and the other?

Granting the necessity of knowledge and of its artistic application in conduct, the question arises as to where the line is to be drawn. Evidently, if anywhere, at specialisms, remote philosophic or mathematical endeavors; life-times spent in inventive attempts without appreciable outcome. But to draw the line is not easy. The remote of one generation is the social tool of the next; the abstract mathematics and physics of the sixteenth and seventeenth centuries are the great social forces of the nineteenth—the locomotive, the telegraph, the telephone, etc. And how, in any case, can we tell a scientific investigator that up to a certain experiment or calculation his work may be social, beyond that, not? All that we can say is that beyond a certain point its social character is not obvious to sense and that the work must be carried on by faith.

Thus it is that we dispose of objections like Bradley's (Ethical Studies, p. 202): "Nothing is easier than to suppose a life of art or speculation which, as far as we can see, though true to itself, has, so far as others are concerned, been sheer waste or even loss, and which knew that it was so." That we can not *see* any social *result* in such cases has nothing to do with the question whether or not the interests themselves are social. We may imagine a life of philanthropic activity, say of devotion to emancipation of slaves in a country wholly given over to slavery, or of a teacher in an unenlightened country, which, as far as we can see, (though, in this case, as in the one referred to by Mr. Bradley, everything depends upon how far we *can* see) has been sheer waste, so far as influence on others is concerned. The point is whether in such cases the life lived is not one of devotion to the interests of humanity as such.

We have been trying to show that everyone admits that science and art, up to a certain point, are social, and that to draw a line where they cease to be so, is in reality to draw a line where we cease to *see* their social character. That we should cease to *see* it, is necessary in the case of almost every advance. Just because the new scientific movement is new, we can realize its social effects only afterwards. But it may be questioned whether the motive which actuates the man of science is not, when fully realized, a *faith* in the social bearing of what he is doing. If we were to go into a metaphysical analysis, the question would have to be raised whether a barely intellectual fact or theory be not a pure abstraction—an unreality if kept apart entirely from the activities of men in relation to one another.

XXXIX.

Science and Art as Necessary Factors of Social Welfare.

Let us consider the problem on its other side. What kind of an interest is our interest in persons, our distinctively social interest? Suppose we attempt to separate our interests in truth, beauty, and use from our interest in persons: *What remains in the persons to be interested in?* Is not a necessary part of out interest in persons, an interest in them as beings fulfilling their respective intellectual and artistic capacities; and if we cut this out of our social interest, have we not maimed and stunted our interest in persons? We wish the fullest life possible to ourselves and to others. And the fullest life means largely a complete and free development of capacities in knowledge and production—production of beauty and use. Our interest in others is not satisfied as long as their intelligence is cramped, their appreciation of truth feeble, their emotions hard and uncomprehensive, their powers of production compressed. To will their true good is to will the freeing of all such gifts to the highest degree. Shall we say that their true good requires that they shall go to the point of understanding algebra, but not quaternions, of understanding ordinary mechanics, but not to working out an electro-magnetic theory of light? to ability to appreciate ordinary chords and and tunes, but not to the attempt to make further developments in music?

And this throws light upon the case referred to by Mr. Bradley. *Social* welfare demands that the individual be permitted to devote himself to the fulfilling of *any* scientific or artistic capacity that he finds within himself—provided, of course, it does not conflict with some more important capacity—irrespective of results. To say to a man: You may devote yourself to this gift, provided you demonstrate beforehand its social bearing, would be to talk nonsense. The new discovery is not yet made. It is absolutely required by the interests of a progressive society that it allow freedom to the individual to develop such functions as he finds in himself, irrespective of any *proved* social effect. Here, as elsewhere, morality works by faith, not by sight.

Indeed the ordinary conception of social interests, of benevolence, needs a large over-hauling. It is practically equivalent to doing something directly for others—to one form or another of charity. But this is only negative morality. A true social interest is that which wills for others freedom from dependence on our *direct* help, which wills to them the self-directed power of exercising, in and by themselves, their own functions. Any will short of this is not social but selfish, willing the dependence of others that we may continue benignly altruistic. The idea of "giving pleasure" to others, "making others happy", if it means anything else than securing conditions so that they may act freely in their own satisfaction, means slavery.

As society advances, social interest must consist more and more in free devotion to intelligence for its own sake, to science, art and industry, and in rejoicing in the exercise of such freedom by others. Meantime, it is truth which makes free.

See Spencer, Data of Ethics, pp. 249–257, where this doctrine is stated with great force.

Where, finally, does the social character of science and art come in? Just here: they are elements in the perfection of individuality, and they are elements whose very nature is to be moving, not rigid; distributed from one to another and not monopolistic possessions. If there are forms of science and art which, at present, are static, being merely owned collections of facts, as one may have a collection of butterflies in a frame, or of etchings in a closed portfolio, this is not because they are science and art, but imperfect science and art. To complete their scientific and artistic character is to set these facts in motion; to hurl them against the world of physical forces till new instruments of man's activity are formed, and to set them in circulation so that others may also participate in their truth and rejoice in their beauty. So far as scientific or artistic attainments are treasured as individual possessions, so far it *is* true that they are not social—but so far it is *also* true that they are immoral: indeed that they are not fully scientific or artistic, being subordinated to having certain sensations.

The intellectual movement of the last four or five centuries has resulted in an infinite specialization in methods, and in an immense accumulation of fact. It is quite true, since the diversity of fact and of method has not yet been brought to an organic unity, that their social bearing is not yet realized. But when the unity is attained (as attained it must be if there is unity in the object of knowledge), it will pass into a corresponding unity of practice. And then the question as to the social character of even the most specialized knowledge will seem absurd. It will be to ask whether men can coöperate better when they do not know than when they do know what they want. Meantime the intellectual confusion, and the resulting divorce of knowledge from practice, exists. But this constitutes a part of the environment of which action must take heed. It makes it one of the pressing duties that every man of intelligence should do his part in bringing out the public and common aspects of knowledge. *The* duty of the present is the socializing of intelligence—the realizing of its bearing upon social practice.

XL.

The Ethical Postulate. We have attempted to show that the various interests are social in their very nature. We have not attempted to show that this can be seen or proved in any given case. On the contrary, in most, if not all cases, the agent acts from a faith that, in realizing his own capacity, he will satisfy the needs of society. If he were asked to *prove* that his devotion to his function were right because certain to promote social good, he might well reply: "That is none of my affair. I have only to work myself out as strength and opportunity are given me, and let the results take care of themselves. I did not make the world, and if it turns out that devotion to the capacity which was given me, and loyalty to the surroundings in which I find myself do not result in good, I do not hold myself responsible. But, after all, I cannot believe that it will so turn out. What is really good for me *must* turn out good for all, or else there is no good in the world at all." The basis, in a word, of moral conduct, with respect to the exercise of function, is a faith that moral self-satisfaction (that is, satisfaction in accordance with the performance of function as already defined) means social satisfaction—or the faith that self and others make a true community. Now such faith or conviction is at the basis of all moral conduct—not simply of the scientific or artistic. Interest in self must mean belief in one's business, conviction of its legitimacy and worth, even prior to any sensible demonstration. Under any circumstances, such demonstration can extend only to past action; the social efficiency of any new end must be a matter of faith. Where such faith is wanting, action becomes halting and character weak. Forcible action fails, and its place is taken by a feeble idealism, of vague longing for that which is not, or by a pessimistic and fruitless discontent with things as they are—leading, in either case, to neglect of actual and pressing duty. The basis of moral strength is *limitation*, the resolve to be one's self only, and to be loyal to the actual powers and surroundings of that self. The saying of Carlyle's about doing the "duty that lies nearest", and of Goethe's that "America is here or nowhere", both imply that faith in the existing moral capacity and environment is the basis of conduct. All fruitful and sound human endeavor roots in the conviction that there is something absolutely worth while, something 'divine' in the demands imposed by one's actual situation and powers. In the great moral heroes of the world the conviction of the worth of their destiny, and of what they were meant to do, has amounted to a kind of fatalism. They have done not simply what they *could* do, but what they *must* do.

On the other hand, effective social interest is based upon what is vaguely called 'faith in humanity', or, more specifically, belief in the value of each man's individuality, belief in some particular function which he might exercise, given appropriate conditions and stimuli. Moral interest in others must be an interest in their possibilities, rather than in their accomplishments; or, better, in their accomplishments so far as these testify to a fulfilling of function—to a working out of capacity. Sympathy and work for men which do not grow out of faith in them are a perfunctory and unfertile sort of thing.

This faith is generally analyzed no further; it is left as faith in one's 'calling' or in 'humanity'. But what is meant is just this: in the performing of such special service as each is capable of, there is to be found not only the satisfaction of self, but also the satisfaction of the entire moral order, the furthering of the community in which one lives. All moral conduct is based upon such a faith; and *moral theory must recognize this as the postulate upon which it rests.* In calling it a postulate, we do not mean that it is a postulate which our theory makes or must make in order to be a theory; but that, through analysis, theory *finds that moral practice makes this postulate*, and that with its reality the reality and value of conduct are bound up.

In calling it a postulate we do not mean to call it unprovable, much less unverifiable, for moral experience is itself, so far as it goes, its verification. But we mean that the further consideration of this postulate, its demonstration or (if the case so be) its refutation, do not belong to the realm of ethics as such. Each branch of human experience rests upon some presupposition which, *for that branch*, is ultimate. The further inquiry into such presuppositions belong not to mathematics, or physics, or ethics, but to metaphysics.

Unless, then, we are to extend our ethical theory to inquire into the possibility and value of moral experience, unless, that is, we are to make an excursion into the metaphysics of ethics, we have here reached our foundation. The ethical postulate, the presupposition involved in conduct, is this:

In the realization of individuality there is found also the needed realization of some community of persons of which the individual is a member; and, conversely, the agent who duly satisfies the community in which he shares, by that same conduct satisfies himself.

Otherwise put, the postulate is that there is a community of persons; a good which realized by the will of one is made not private but public. It is this unity of individuals as respects the end of action, this existence of a practical common good, that makes what we call the moral order of the world.

Shakespeare has stated the postulate—

To thine ownself be true;
And it must follow, as the night the day,
Thou can'st not then be false to any man.

Its significance may be further developed by comparing it with the scientific postulate.

All science rests upon the conviction of the thorough-going and permanent unity of the world of objects known—a unity which is sometimes termed the 'uniformity of nature' or the 'reign of law'; without this conviction that objects are not mere isolated and transitory appearances, but are connected together in a system by laws or relations, science would be an impossibility. Moral experience *makes for the world of practice* an assumption analogous in kind to that which intellectual experience makes for the world of knowledge. And just as it is not the affair of science, as such, or even of logic (the theory of science) to justify this presupposition of science, or to do more than show its presence in intellectual experience, so it is not the business of conduct, or even of ethics (the theory of conduct) to justify what we have termed the 'ethical postulate'. In each case the further inquiry belongs to metaphysics.

XLI.

Does the End Proposed Serve as a Criterion of Conduct?

We have now concluded that an end which may be termed indifferently 'The Realization of Individuality', 'The Performance of Specific Functions', 'The Satisfaction of Interests', 'The Realization of a Community of Individuals' is the moral end. Will this end serve the two aims (see Sec. XVI) required of a criterion, or standard: (1) Will it unify individual conduct? (2) Will it afford a common good? We have just been endeavoring to show that it does both of these things; that as the realization of one's specific capacity, it unifies individual conduct, and that, as the performance of function, it serves to satisfy the entire community. To take up just these points, accordingly, would involve a repetition of what has been said, and we shall therefore take up instead some aspects of the individual and social unity of conduct, not already considered.

1. The System of Individual Conduct. We must be careful not to interpret the idea of specific function too rigidly or abstractly. It does not mean that each one has some supreme mission in life to which everything else must be sacrificed—that a man is to be an artist, or a soldier, or a student, or a day-laborer and nothing else. On the contrary, the idea of function is that which comprehends all the various sides of life, and it cannot be narrowed below the meaning we have already given: the due adjustment of capacity and surroundings. Wherever there is any capacity or any circumstance, no matter how trivial, there is something included in the exercise of function, and, therefore to be satisfied—according to its place, of course, in the whole of life. Amusements and all the minor details of life are included within the scope of morality. They are elements in the exercise of function, and their insignificance and triviality does not exclude them from the grasp of duty and of the good. It is a mistake to suppose that because it is optional or indifferent—as it constantly is—what acts among the minor details of life are to be done or left undone, or unimportant whether they are done or left undone at all, therefore such acts have no moral value. Morality con-

sists in treating them just as they are—if they are slight or trivial they are to be performed as slight and trivial. Morality does not simply permit the performance of such acts, but demands it. To try to make, in the interests of duty, a serious matter out of every detail of life would be immoral—as much so, in kind, as to make light of momentous matters.

See Alexander, Op. cit. pp. 53-54.
Bradley, Op. cit., pp. 194-197.

Consider, also, how this conception of the end stands in definite relation to concrete acts; how it explains the possibility of decision as to whether this or that proposed act is right. We do not have to trace the connection of the act with some end beyond, as pleasure, or abstract law. We have only to analyze the *act itself.* We have certain definite and wholly concrete facts; the given capacity of the person at the given moment, and his given surroundings. The judgment as to the nature of these facts is, in and of itself, a judgment as to the act to be done. The question is not: What is the probability that this act will result in the balance of maximum pleasure; it is not what general rule can we hunt up under which to bring this case. It is simply: *What is this case?* The moral act is not that which satisfies some far away principle, hedonistic or transcendental. It is that which meets the present, actual situation. Difficulties indeed, arise, but they are simply the difficulty of resolving a complex case; they are intellectual, not moral. The case made out, the moral end stands forth. No extraneous manipulation, to bring the case under some foreign end, is required.

And this suggests the elasticity of the criterion. In fact moral conduct is entirely individualized. It is where, when, how and of whom. There has been much useless discussion as to the absolute or relative character of morals—useless because the terms absolute and relative are not defined. If absolute is taken to mean immobile and rigid, it is anything but desirable that morals should be absolute. If the physical world is a scene of movement, in which there is no rest, it is a poor compliment to pay the moral world to conceive of it as static and lifeless. A rigid criterion in a world of developing social relations would speedily prove no criterion at all. It would be an abstract rule, taking no account of the individualized character of each act; its individuality of capacity and of surroundings, of time, place and relationships involved. A truly absolute criterion is one which adjusts itself to each case according to the specific nature of the case; one which moves with the moving world. On the other hand, if relative means uncertain in application, changing in time and place without reason for change in the facts themselves, then certainly the criterion is not relative. If it means taking note of all concrete relations involved, it *is* relative. The absoluteness, in fine, of the standard of action consists not in some rigid statement, but in never-failing application. Universality here, as elsewhere, resides not in a thing, but in a way, a method of action. The absolute standard is the one applicable to all deeds, and the conception of the exercise of function is thus absolute, covering all conduct from the mainly impulsive action of the savage to the most complex reaches of modern life.

Aristotle's well known theory of the 'mean' seems to have its bearing here. "It is possible," he says (Peters' trans. of Ethics, p. 46), "to feel fear, confidence, desire, anger, pity, and generally to be affected pleasantly and painfully, either too much or too little—in either case wrongfully; but to be affected thus at the right *times*, and on the right *occasions*, and toward the right *persons*, and with the right *object* and in the right *fashions*, is the mean course and the best course, and these are characteristics of virtue." The right time, occasion, person, purpose and fashion—what is it but the complete individualization of conduct in order to meet the whole demands of the whole situation, instead of some abstraction? And what else do we mean by fit, due, proper, right action, but that which just hits the mark, without falling short or deflecting, and, to mix the metaphor, without slopping over?

2. The system of social conduct, or common good. Moral conduct springs from the faith that

all right action is social and its purpose is to justify this faith by working out the social values involved. The term 'moral community' can mean only a unity of action, made what it is by the coöperating activities of diverse individuals. There is unity in the work of a factory, not in spite of, but *because of* the division of labor. Each workman forms the unity not by doing the same that everybody else does, or by trying to do the whole, but by doing his specific part. The unity is the one activity which their varied activities make. And so it is with the moral activity of society and the activities of individuals. The more individualized the functions, the more perfect the unity. (See section LII.)

The exercise of function by an agent serves, then, both to define and to unite him. It makes him a *distinct* social member at the same time that it makes him a *member*. Possession of peculiar capacities, and special surroundings mark one person off from another and make him an individual; and the due adjustment of capacities to surroundings (in the exercise of function) effects, therefore, the realization of individuality—the realization of what we specifically are as distinct from others. At the same time, this distinction is not isolation; the exercise of function is the performing of a special *service* without which the social whole is defective. Individuality means not separation, but defined position in a whole; special aptitude in constituting the whole.

We are now in a position to take up the consideration of the two other fundamental ethical conceptions—obligation and freedom. These ideas answer respectively to the two sides of the exercise of function. On the one hand, the performing of a function realizes the social whole. Man is thus 'bound' by the relations necessary to constitute this whole. He is subject to the conditions which the existence and growth of the social unity impose. He is, in a word, under *obligation;* the performance of his function is duty owed to the community of which he is a member.

But on the other hand, activity in the way of function realizes the individual; it is what makes him an individual, or distinct person. In the performance of his own function the agent satisfies his own interests and gains power. In it is found his *freedom.*

Obligation thus corresponds to the *social* satisfaction, freedom to the *self*-satisfaction, involved in the exercise of function; and they can no more be separated from each other than the correlative satisfaction can be. One has to realize himself as a member of a community. In this fact are found both freedom and duty.

Chapter II.—THE IDEA OF OBLIGATION.

XLII.

Theories Regarding Moral Authority. The idea of obligation or duty has two sides. There is the idea of law, of something which controls conduct, and there is the *consciousness* of the necessity of conforming to this law. There is, of course, no separation between the two sides, but the consideration of the latter side—the recognition of obligation—may be best dealt with in discussing conscience. Here we shall deal simply with the fact that there is such a thing in conduct as law controlling action, and constituting obligation. Theories regarding obligation may, for our purposes, be subdivided into those which make its exercise restraint or coercion (and which therefore hold that in perfect moral conduct, duty as such disappears); and those which hold that obligation is a normal element in conduct as such, and that it is not, essentially, but only under certain circumstances, coercive. Of the former type, some theories (mainly the hedonistic) regard the restraint as originally imposed from without upon the desires of the individual, while others (as the Kantian) regard it as imposed by man's reason upon his desires and inclinations.

XLIII.

Bain's Theory of Obligation.

It is obvious that the question of obligation presents considerable difficulty to the hedonistic school. If the end of conduct is pleasure, as the satisfaction of desire, why should not each desire be satisfied, if possible, as it arises, and thus pleasure secured? What meaning is there in the term 'duty' or 'obligation' if the moral end or good coincides wholly with the natural end of the inclinations themselves? It is evident, at all events, that the term can have significance only if there is some cause preventing the desires as they arise from natural satisfaction. The problem of obligation in hedonism thus becomes the problem of discovering that outside force which restrains, or, at least, constrains, the desire from immediate gratification. According to Bain, this outside force is social disapprobation manifested through the form of punishment.

"I consider that the proper meaning, or import of the terms [duty, obligation] refers to that class of action which is enforced by the sanction of punishment. . . . . The powers that impose the obligatory sanction are Law and Society, or the community acting through the Government by public judicial acts, and apart from the Government by the unofficial expressions of disapprobation and the exclusion from social good offices". Emotions and Will, p. 286. See also pp. 321–323 and p. 527.

Through this 'actual and ideal avoidance of certain acts and dread of punishment' the individual learns to forego the gratification of some of his natural impulses, and learns also to cultivate and even to originate desires not at first spontaneous. "The child is open from the first to the blame and praise of others, and thus is led to do or avoid certain acts".

On the model, however, of the action of this external authority there grows up, in time an internal authority—"an ideal resemblance of public authority" (p. 287), or "a *fac simile* of the system of government around us" (p. 313).

"The sentiment, at first formed and cultivated by the relations of actual command and obedience, may come at last to stand upon an independent foundation. . . . . . When the young mind, accustomed at the outset to implicitly obeying any set of rules is sufficiently advanced to appreciate the motive—the utilities or the sentiment that led to their imposition — the character of the conscience is entirely changed. . . . . Regard is now had to the intent and meaning of the law, and not to the mere fact of its being prescribed by some power" (E. and W., p. 318).

But when the sense of obligation becomes entirely detached from the social sanction, "even then the notion, sentiment or form of duty is derived from what society imposes, although the particular matter is quite different. Social obligation develops in the mind originally the feeling and habit of obligation, and this remains although the particular articles are changed" (page 319, note). *Cf.* also Bain, Moral Science, pp. 20-21 and 41-43.

XLIV.

Spencer's Theory of Obligation. Spencer's theory is, in substance, an enlarged and better analyzed restatement of Bain's theory. Bain nowhere clearly states in what the essence of obligation consists, when it becomes independent, when the internal *fac simile* is formed. *Why* should I not gratify my desires as I please in case social pressure is absent or lets up? Spencer supplies the missing element. According to him, "the essential trait in the moral consciousness is the control of some feeling or feelings by some other feeling or feelings" (Data of Ethics, p. 113). The kind of feeling which controls is that which is more complex and which relates to more remote ends; or, we are 'obliged' to give up more immediate, special and direct pleasures for the sake of securing more general, remote and indirect ones. Obligation, in its essence, is the surrender or subordination of present to future satisfaction. This control, restraint, or suppression may be 'independent' or, self-imposed, but is not so at first, either in the man or in the child. Prior to self-restraint are the restraints imposed by the "visible ruler, the invisible ruler and society at large"—the policeman, the priest and public opinion. The man is induced to postpone immediate gratification through his fear of others, especially of the chief, of the dead and of social displeasure — "legal penalty, supernatural punishment and social reprobation". Thus there grows up the sense of obligation. This refers at first only to the above-mentioned extrinsic effects of action. But finally the mind learns to consider the intrinsic effect of the action itself—the evil inflicted by the evil deed, and then the sense of duty, or coercion, evolved through the aforesaid external agencies, becomes transferred to this new mode of controlling action. Desires are now controlled through considerations of what their *own* effects would be, were the desires acted upon.

It follows "that the sense of duty or moral obligation is transitory, and will diminish as fast as moralization increases" (page 127). Even when compulsion is self-imposed, there is still compulsion, coercion, and this must be done away with. It *is* done away with as far as an act which is at first done only for the sake of its own remoter consequences comes to be done for its own sake. And this will ultimately occur, if the act is continued, since "persistence in performing a duty ends in making it a pleasure".

See Guyau, La Morale Anglaise Contemporaine, besides the works of Bain and Spencer. In addition to objections which will forthwith be made, we may here note a false abstraction of Spencer's. He makes the act and its consequences *two* things, while the act and its consequences (provided they are known as such) are the same thing, no matter whether consequences are near or remote. The only distinction is that consequences once not known as such at all are seen in time to be really consequences, and thus to be part of the content of the act. The transfer from the "external consequences" imposed by the ruler, priest and public-opinion to the intrinsic consequences of the act itself, is thus a transfer from an immoral to a moral basis. This is very different from a change of the form of obligation itself.

XLV.

Criticism of these Theories. Putting aside the consideration of the relation of desire to duty, (the question whether duty is essentially coercive) until after we have taken up the Kantian idea of obligation, we may note the following objections to the theories just stated. Their great defect is that they do not give us any method of differentiating moral coercion (or obligation) from the action of mere superior physical force. Taking it (first) upon the side of the individual: Is there any reason *why* the individual submits to the external authority of government except that he *has* to do so? He may argue that, since others possess superior force, he will avoid certain pains by conforming to their demands, but such yielding, whether temporary or permanent, to superior force is very far from being a recognition that one *ought* to act as the superior force dictates. The theories must logically commit us to the doctrine that 'might makes right' in its baldest form. Every one knows that, when the individual surrenders the natural gratifications of his desires to the command of others, if his sole reason is the superior force of the commanding party, he does not forego in the surrender his right to such gratification the moment he has the chance to get it. Actual slavery would be the model school of duties, if these theories were true.

The facts adduced by Bain and Spencer—the growth of the recognition of duties in the child through the authority of the parents, and in the savage through the use of authority by the chief—are real enough, but what they prove is that obligation may be brought home to one by force, not that force creates obligation. The child and the man yield to force in such a way that their sense of duty is developed only in case they recognize, implicitly, the force or the authority as already *right*. Let it be recognized that *rightful* force (as distinct from mere brute strength) resides in certain social authorities, and these social authorities may do much, beyond the shadow of doubt, to give effect to the special deeds and relations which are to be considered obligatory. These theories, in fine, take the fact of obligation for granted, and, at most, only show the historical process by which its fuller recognition is brought about. Force in the service of right is one thing ; force as constituting and creating right is another.

And this is to say (secondly), considering the matter from the side of society, that the theories of Bain and Spencer do not explain why or how social authority should exercise coercive force over the individual. If it is implied that they do so in the moral interests of the individual or of the community, this takes it for granted that there already is in existence a moral ideal obligatory upon the individual. If it is implied that they exercise coercive force in the interests of their own private pleasure, this might establish a despotism, or lead to a political revolt, but it is difficult to see how it could create the fact of duty. When we consider any concrete case, we see that society, in its compelling of the individual, is possessed of moral ideals; and that it conceives itself not merely as having the *power* to make the individual conform to them, nor as having the *right* merely; but as under the bounden *duty* of bringing home to the individual *his* duties. The social authorities do not, perforce, create morality, but they embody and make effective the existing morality. It is only just because the actions which they impose are thought of as *good*, good for others as for themselves, that this imposition is taken out of the realm of tyranny into that of duty (see Sec. XXXVIII).

XLVI.

The Kantian Theory of Obligation. As we have seen, Kant takes the conception of duty as the primary ethical notion, superior to that of the good, and places it in the most abrupt opposition to desire. The relation of duty to desire is not control of some feelings by others, but rather suppression of all desire (not in itself, but as a *motive* of action) in favor of the consciousness of law universal. We have, on one side, according to Kant, the desire and inclination, which are sensuous and pathological. These constitute man's 'lower nature'. On the other side there is Reason, which is essentially universal, above all caprice and all prostitution to private pleasure. This Reason, or 'higher nature', imposes a law upon the sentient being of man, a law which takes the form of a command (the 'Categorical Imperative'). This relation of a higher rational nature issuing commands to a lower sensuous nature (both within man himself), is the very essence of duty. If man were wholly a sentient being, he would have only to follow his natural impulses, like the animals. If he were only a rational being, he would necessarily obey his reason, and there would still be no talk of obligation. But because of the dualism, because of the absolute opposition between Reason and Desire, man is a being subject to obligation.

Reason says to the desires "Thou shalt" or "Thou shalt not". Yet this obligation is not externally imposed; the man as rational imposes it upon himself as sensuous. Thus Kant says that, in the realm of morality, man is both sovereign and subject.

The reflex influence of Rousseau's social theories upon Kant's moral doctrines in this respect is worthy of more attention than it usually receives. Kant's moral theory is hardly more than a translation of Rousseau's politics into ethical terms, through its union with Kant's previously established dualism of reason and sense.

XLVII.

Criticism of the Kantian Theory.

1. No one can deny that a genuine opposition exists between the 'natural' desires and moral activity. The being that satisfies each desire or appetite as it arises, without reference of it to, or control of it by, some principle, has not had the horizon of conduct lift before him. But Kant makes the satisfaction of desire *as such* (not of this or that desire) antagonistic to action from duty. Kant was forced into this position by his fundamental division of sense from reason, but it carries with it its own condemnation and thus that of the premises from which it is derived. It comes to saying that the actual desires and appetites are not what they ought to be. This, in itself,

is true enough. But when Kant goes on to say, as he virtually does, that what ought to be *cannot* be, that the desires as such cannot be brought into harmony with principle, he has made the moral life not only a riddle, but a riddle with no answer. If mankind were once convinced that the moral ideal were something which ought to be but which could not be, we may easily imagine how much longer moral endeavor would continue. The first or immediate stimulus to moral effort is the conviction that the desires and appetites are not what they should be; the underlying and continuing stimulus is the conviction that the expression of desires in harmony with law is the sole abiding good of man. To reconcile the two is the very meaning of the moral struggle (see Sec. LXIV). Strictly, according to Kant, morality would either leave the appetites untouched or would abolish them—in either case destroying morality.

See Caird, Op. cit., Vol. II, pp. 226–28.

2. Kant again seems to be on the right track in declaring that obligation is not anything externally imposed, but is the law of man's being, self-imposed. This principle of 'autonomy' is the only escape from a theory of obligation which would make obligation external, and regard for it slavish fear, or servile hope of reward. To regard even a Divine Being as the author of obligation is

to make it a form of external constraint, appealing only to hope or fear, unless this Divine Being is shown to be organically connected with self.

But this abstract universal reason which somehow dwells, without mediation or reason, in each individual, seems to be somewhat scholastic, a trifle mythological. There is undoubtedly in man's experience a function which corresponds to what Kant is aiming, thus mythologically, to describe. But it is one thing to recognize an opposition of a desire, in its isolation, to desire as organic to the function of the whole man; it is another to split man into a blank dualism of an abstract reason, on one side, having no antecedents or bearings, and of a mess of appetites, having only animal relationship, on the other. The truth that Kant is aiming to preserve seems to be fairly stated as two-fold: first, that duty is self-imposed, and thus the dutiful will autonomous or free; and, second, the presence of struggle in man between a 'lower' and a 'higher'. The first point seems to be sufficiently met by the idea already advanced that self, or individuality, is essentially social, being constituted not by isolated capacity, but by capacity acting in response to the needs of an environment—an environment which, when taken in its fullness, is a community of persons. Any law imposed by such a self would be 'universal', but this universality would not be an isolated possession of the individual; it would be another name for the concrete social relationships which make the individual what he is, as a social member or organ. Furthermore, such a universal law would not be formal, but would have a content—these same relationships.

The second point seems to be met by recognizing that in the realization of the law of social function, conflict must occur between the desire as an immediate and direct expression of the individual—the desire in its isolation—and desire as an expression of the whole man; desire, that is, as wholly conformable to the needs of the surroundings. Such a conflict is real enough, as everyone's experience will testify, but it is a conflict which may be solved—which must be solved so far as morality is attained. And since it is a conflict within desire itself, its solution or morality, does not require any impossible obliteration of desire, nor any acting from an 'ought' which has no relation to what 'is'. This, indeed, is *the* failure of the Kantian Ethics: in separating what should be from what is, it deprives the latter, the existing social world as well as the desires of the individual, of all moral value; while, by the same separation, it condemns that which should be to a barren abstraction. An 'ought' which does not root in and flower from the 'is', which is not the fuller realization of the actual state of social relationships, is a mere pious wish that things should be better. And morality, that is, right action, is not so feeble as this would come to.

XLVIII.

The Source and Nature of Obligation. The basis of a correct theory of obligation lies, as already stated, in holding fast to its concrete relations to the moral end, or good. This end consists in an activity in which capacity is exercised in accordance with surroundings, with the social needs which affect the individual. It is implied in this very idea, that the end is not something which the individual may set up at his own arbitrary will. The social needs give control, law, authority. The individual may not manifest his capacity, satisfy his desires, apart from their specific relation to the environment in which they exist. The general fact of obligation which is constituted through this control of capacity by the wider function is, of course, differentiated into specific 'laws' or duties by the various forms which the one function takes, as capacity and circumstances vary.

In other words, obligation or duty is simply the aspect which the good or the moral end assumes, as the individual conceives of it. From the very fact that the end is the good, and yet is not realized by the individual, it presents itself to him as that which *should be realized*—as the ideal of action. It requires no further argument to show that obligation is at once self-imposed, and social in its content. It is self-imposed because it flows from the good, from the idea of the full activity of the individual's own will. It is no law imposed from without; but is his own law, the law of his own function, of his individuality. Its social content flows from the fact that this individuality is not mere capacity, but is this capacity *acting*, and acting so as to comprehend social relationships.

Suppose that man's good and his conviction of duty were divorced from one another—that man's duty were other than to fulfill his own specific function. Such a thing would make duty purely formal; the moral law would have no intrinsic relation to daily conduct, to the expression of man's powers and wants. There have, indeed, been moralists who think they do the Lord service, who think they add to the dignity and sacredness of Duty by making it other than the idea of the activity of man, regulated indeed, but regulated only by its own principle of activity. But such moralists in their desire to consecrate the idea of duty remove from it all content, and leave it an empty abstraction. On the other hand, their eagerness to give absoluteness and imperativeness to duty by making it a law other than that of the normal expression of man, casts discredit upon the one moral reality—the full, free play of human life. In denying that duty is simply the *intrinsic* law, the *self*-manifestation of this life, they make this life immoral, or at least non-moral. They degrade it to a bundle of appetites and powers having no moral value until the outside moral law is applied to them. In reality, the dignity and imperativeness of duty are simply the manifest dignity and unconditioned worth of human life as exhibited in its free activity. The whole idea of the separateness of duty from the concrete flow of human action is a virulent example of the fallacy mentioned in an early section—the fallacy that moral action means something more than action itself (see Sec. II).

The attempt to act upon a theory of the divorce of satisfaction and duty, to carry it out in practice, means the maiming of desire through distrust of its moral significance, and thus, by withdrawing the impetus of action, the reduction of life to mere passivity. So far as this does not happen, it means the erection of the struggle itself, the erection of the opposition of law to desire, into the very principle of the moral life. The essential principle of the moral life, that good consists in the freeing of impulse, of appetite, of desire, of power, by enabling them to flow in the channel of a unified and full end is lost sight of, and the free service of the spirit is reduced to the slavish fear of a bond-man under a hard taskmaster.

The essential point in the analysis of moral law, or obligation, having been found, we may briefly discuss some subsidiary points.

1. The relation of duty to a given desire. As any desire arises, it will be, except so far as character has already been moralized, a demand for its own satisfaction; the desire, in a word, will be isolated. In so far, duty will be in a negative attitude towards the desire; it will insist first upon its limitation, and then upon its transformation. So far as it is merely limitative, it demands the denying of the desire, and so far assumes a coercive form. But this limitation is not for its own sake, but for that of the transformation of desire into a freer and more adequate form—into a form, that is, where it will carry with it, when it passes into action, *more of activity*, than the original desire would have done.

Does duty itself disappear when its constraint disappears? On the contrary, so far as an act is done unwillingly, under constraint, so far the act is impure, and *undutiful*. The very fact that there is need of constraint shows that the self is divided; that there is a two-fold interest and purpose—one in the law of the activity according to function, the other in the special end of the particular desire. Let the act be done *wholly as duty*, and it is done wholly for its own sake; love, passion take the place of constraint. This suggests:

2. Duty for duty's sake.

It is clear that such an expression states a real moral fact; unless a duty is done *as* duty it is not done morally. An act may be outwardly just what what morality demands, and yet if done for the sake of some private advantage it is not counted moral. As Kant expresses it, an act must be done not only in accordance with duty, but *from duty.* This truth, however, is misinterpreted when it is taken to mean that the act is to be done for the sake of duty, and duty is conceived as a third thing outside the act itself. Such a theory contradicts the true sense of the phrase 'duty for duty's sake', for it makes the act done not for its own sake, but as a mere means to an abstract law beyond itself. 'Do the right because it is the right' means do the right *thing* because it *is* the right thing; that is, do the act disinterestedly from interest in the act itself. A duty is always some act or line of action, not a third thing outside the act to which it is to conform. In short, duty means *the act which is to be done*, and 'duty for duty's sake' means do the required act as it really is; do not degrade it into a means for some ulterior end. This is as true in practice as in theory. A man who does his duty not for the sake of the acts themselves, but for the sake of some abstract 'ideal' which he christens duty in general, will have a morality at once hard and barren, and weak and sentimental.

3. The agency of moral authority in prescribing moral law and stimulating to moral conduct.

The facts, relied upon by Bain and Spencer, as to the part played by social influences in imposing duties, are undeniable. The facts, however, are unaccountable upon the theory of these writers, as that theory would, as we have seen, explain only the influence of society in producing acts done from fear or for hope of reward. But if the individual and others are equally members of one society, if the performance by each man of his own function constitutes a good common to all, it is inevitable that social authorities should be an influence in constituting and teaching duties. The community, in imposing its own needs and demands upon the individual, is simply arousing him to a knowledge of his relationships in life, to a knowledge of the moral environment in which he lives, and of the acts which he must perform if he is to realize his individuality. The community in awakening moral consciousness in the morally immature may appeal to motives of hope and fear. But even this fact does not mean that to the child, duty is necessarily constituted by fear of punishment or hope of reward. It means simply that his capacity and his surroundings are both so undeveloped that the exercise of his function takes mainly the form of pleasing others. He may still do his duty *as* his duty, but his duty now consists in pleasing others.

On Obligation see Green, Op. cit., pp. 352–356; Alexander, Op. cit., pp. 142–147. For different views, Martineau, Op. cit., Vol. II, pp. 92–119; Calderwood, Op. cit., pp. 131–138, and see also, Grote, Treatise on Moral Ideals, ch. VII.

Chapter III.—THE IDEA OF FREEDOM.

XLIX.

The Forms of Freedom. We may now deal, more briefly, with the problem of moral capacity. It is, in principle, the ability to conceive of an end and to be governed in action by this conceived end. We may consider this capacity in three aspects, as negative, as potential and as positive.

1. *Negative Aspect of Freedom.* The power to be governed in action by the thought of some end to be reached is freedom *from* the appetites and desires. An animal which does not have the power of proposing ends to itself is impelled to action by its wants and appetites just as they come into con-

sciousness. It is *irritated* into acting. Each impulse demands its own satisfaction, and the animal is helpless to rise above the particular want. But a *person*, one who can direct his action by conscious ends, is emancipated from subjection to the particular appetites. He can consider their relation to the end which he has set before himself, and can reject, modify or use them as best agrees with the purposed end. This capacity to control and subjugate impulses by reflection upon their relationship to a rational end is the power of self-government, and the more distinct and the more comprehensive in scope the end is, the more real the self-government.

2. *Potential Freedom.* The power to conceive of ends involves the possibility of thinking of many and various ends, and even of ends which are contrary to one another. If an agent could conceive of but one end in some case, it would always seem to him afterwards that he had been necessitated to act in the direction of that end; but the power to put various ends before self constitutes "freedom of choice", or potential freedom. After action, the agent calls to mind that there was another end open to him, and that if he did not choose the other end, it was because of something in his character which made him prefer the one he actually chose.

L.

Moral Responsibility. Here we have the basis of moral *responsibility* or *accountability.* There is no responsibility for any result which is not intended or foreseen. Such a consequence is only physical, not moral. (Sec. VII). But when any result has been foreseen, and adopted as foreseen, such result is the outcome not of any external circumstances, nor of mere desires and impulses, but of the agent's conception of his own end. Now, because the result thus flows from the agent's own conception of an end, he feels himself responsible for it.

It must be remembered that the end adopted is that which is conceived *as satisfying self*—that, indeed, when we say end of action, we mean only some proposed form of self-satisfaction. The adopted end always indicates, therefore, that sort of condition which the agent considers to be good, or self-satisfactory. It is because a result flows from the agent's *ideal of himself*, the thought of himself which he considers desirable or worth realizing, that the agent feels himself responsible. The result is simply an expression of himself; a manifestation of what he would have himself be. Responsibility is thus one aspect of the identity of character and conduct. (Sec. VII). We are responsible for our conduct because that conduct is ourselves objectified in actions.

The idea of responsibility is intensified whenever there have been two contrary lines of conduct conceived, of which one has been chosen. If the end adopted turns out not to be satisfactory, but, rather, unworthy and degrading, the agent feels that he *might* have chosen the other end, and that if he did not, it was because his character was such, his ideal of himself was such, that this other end did not appeal to him. The actual result is felt to be the outcome of an unworthy character manifested in the adoption of a low form of satisfaction; and the evident contrast of this low form with a higher form, present to consciousness but rejected, makes the sense of responsibility more acute. As such, it is the judgment of disapprobation passed upon conduct; the feeling of remorse and of the desert of punishment. Freedom as the power of conceiving ends and of realizing the ideal end in action, is thus the basis both of responsibility and of approbation (or disapprobation).

The Freedom of Indifference. It is this potential freedom, arising from the power of proposing various ends of action, which, misinterpreted, gives rise to the theory of a liberty of indifferent choice—the theory that the agent can choose this or that without any ground or motive. The real experience is the knowledge, after the choice of one end, that since another end was also present to consciousness that other end might have been chosen, *if only the character had been such as to find its satisfaction in that other end.* The theory of indifference misconstrues this fact to mean that the agent might just as well have chosen that other end, without any if or qualification whatever. The theory of indifference, moreover, defeats its own end. The point which it is anxious to save is responsibility. It sees that if only one course of action were ever open to an agent, without the possibility of any *conception* of another course, an agent, so acting, could not be held responsible for not having adopted that other course. And so it argues that there must always be the possibility of indifferent or alternate choice; the possibility of adopting this or that line of action without any motive. But if such were the case responsibility would be destroyed. If the end chosen is not an expression of character, if it does not manifest the agent's ideal of himself, if its choice is a matter of indifference, it does not signify morally, but is mere accident or caprice. It is because choice is *not* a matter of indifference, but an outcome of character that the agent feels responsibility, and approves or disapproves. He virtually says: "I am responsible for this outcome, not because I could have chosen another end just as well *without any reason,* but because I thought of another end and rejected it; because my character was such that that end did not seem good, and was such that this end did seem good. My character is myself, and in this unworthy end I stand self-condemned."

LI.

Moral Reformation. Freedom considered as potential, depending upon the power of the agent to frame diverse ends, is the basis not only of responsibility, but also of the possibility of reformation, or of change in character and conduct. All moral action is the expression of self, but the self is not something fixed or rigid. It includes as a necessary part of itself the possibility of framing conceptions of what it would be, and there is, therefore, at any time the possibility of acting upon some ideal hitherto unrealized. If conduct were the expression of character, in a sense which identified character wholly with past attainments, then reformation would be impossible. What a man once was he must always continue to be. But past attainments do not exhaust all the possibilities of character. Since conduct necessarily implies a continuous adjustment of developing capacity to new conditions, there is the ability to frame a changed ideal of self-satisfaction —that is, ability to lead a new life. That the new ideal is adopted from experience of the unworthy nature of former deeds is what we should expect. The chosen end having proved itself unsatisfactory, the alternative end, previously rejected, recurs to consciousness with added claims. To sum up: The doctrine that choice depends upon character is correct, but the doctrine is misused when taken to mean that a man's outward conduct will always be in the same direction that it has been. Character involves all the ideas of different and of better things which have been present to the agent, although he has never attempted to carry them out. And there is always the possibility that, if the proper influences are brought to bear, some one of these latent ideals may be made vital, and wholly change the bent of character and of conduct.

LII.

Positive Freedom. The *capacity* of freedom lies in the power to form an ideal or conception of an end. *Actual* freedom lies in the realization of that end which actually satisfies. An end may be freely adopted, and yet its actual working out may result not in freedom, but in slavery. It may result in rendering the agent more subject to his passions, less able to direct his own conduct, and more cramped and feeble in powers. Only that end which executed really effects greater energy and comprehensiveness of character makes for actual freedom. In a word, only the good man, the man who is truly realizing his individuality, is free, in the positive sense of that word.

Every action which is not in the line of performance of functions must necessarily result in self enslavement. The end of desire is activity; and it is only in fullness and unity of activity that freedom is found. When desires are not unified—when, that is, the idea of the exercise of function does not control conduct—one desire must conflict with another. Action is directed now this way, now that, and there is friction, loss of power. On account of this same lack of control of desires by the comprehensive law of social activity, one member of society is brought into conflict with another, with waste of energy, and with impeded and divided activity and satisfaction of desire. Exercise of function, on the other hand, unifies the desires, giving each its relative, although subordinate, place. It fits each into the others, and, through the harmonious adjustment of one to another, effects that complete and unhindered action which is freedom. The performance of specific function falls also into free relations with the activities of other persons, coöperating with them, giving and receiving what is needed, and thus constituting full liberty. Other aspects of freedom, as the negative and the potential, are simply means instrumental to the realization of individuality, and when not employed toward this, their true end, they become methods of enslaving the agent.

On the subject of moral freedom, as, upon the whole, in agreement with the view presented here: See

Green: Prolegomena to Ethics, pp. 90–117; 142–158. Bradley: Ethical Studies, ch. I; Caird: Phil. of Kant, Vol. II, Bk. II, ch. 3; Alexander: Moral Order and Progress, pp. 336–341.

And, for a view agreeing in part, Stephen: Science of Ethics, pp. 278–293.

For presentations of the freedom of indifference,

see, Lotze: Practical Philosophy, ch. 3. Martineau: Op. cit., Vol. II, pp. 34–40. Calderwood: Handbook of Moral Philosophy.

PART II.

THE ETHICAL WORLD.

LIII.

The Reality of Moral Relations.

The habit of conceiving moral action as a certain *kind* of action, instead of all action so far as it really is action, leads us to conceive of morality as a highly desirable something which somehow ought to be brought into our lives, but which upon the whole is not. It gives rise to the habit of conceiving morality as a vague ideal which it is praiseworthy for the individual to strive for, but which depends wholly for its existence upon the individual's wish in the matter. Morality, that is, is considered as a relation existing between something which merely *ought to be*, on one hand, and the individual's choice, or his conscience on the other. This point of view has found typical expression in Bishop Butler's saying: "If conscience had might as it has right, it would rule the world."

But right is not such a helpless creature. It exists not in word but in power. The moral world is, here and now; it is a reality apart from the wishes, or failures to wish, of any given individual. It bears the same relation to the individual's activity that the 'physical world' does to his knowledge. Not till the individual has to spin the physical world out of his consciousness in order to know it, will it be necessary for him to create morality by his choice, before it can exist. As knowledge is mastery in one's self of the real world, the reproduction of it in self-consciousness, so moral action is the appropriation and vital self-expression of the values contained in the existing practical world.

The existence of this moral world is not anything vaguely mysterious. Imagine a well organized factory, in which there is some comprehensive industry carried on—say the production of cotton cloth. This is the end; it is a common end—that for which each individual labors. Not all individuals, however, are doing the same thing. The more perfect the activity, the better organized the work, the more differentiated their respective labors. This is the side of individual activity or freedom. To make the analogy with moral activity complete we have to suppose that each individual is doing the work because of itself, and not merely as drudgery for the sake of some further end, as pay. Now these various individuals are bound together by their various acts; some more nearly because doing closely allied things, all somewhat, because contributing to a common activity. This is the side of laws and duties.

This group of the differentiated and yet related activities is the analogue of the moral world. There are certain wants which have constantly to be fulfilled; certain ends which demand coöperating activities, and which establish fixed relations between men. There is a world of ends, a realm of definite activities in existence, as concrete as the ends and activities in our imagined factory. The child finds, then, ends and actions in existence when he is born. More than this: he is not born as a mere spectator of the world; he is born *into* it. He finds himself encompassed by such relations, and he finds his own being and activity intermeshed with them. If he takes away from himself, as an agent, what he has, as sharing in these ends and actions, nothing remains.

LIV.

Moral Institutions. This world of purposes and activities is differentiated into various institutions. The child is born as a member of a *family;* as he grows up he finds that others have possessions which he must respect, that is, he runs upon the institution of *property.* As he grows still older, he finds persons outside of the family of whose actions he must take account as respects his own: *society,* in the limited sense as meaning relations of special intimacy or acquaintanceship. Then he finds the political institutions; the city, state and nation. He finds an educational institution, the school, the college; religious institutions, the church, etc., etc. Everywhere he finds men having common wants and thus proposing common ends and using coöperative modes of action. To these organized modes of action, with their reference to common interests and purposes, he must adjust his activities; he must take his part therein, if he acts at all, though it be only negatively or hostilely, as in evil conduct. These institutions *are* morality real and objective; the individual becomes moral as he shares in this moral world, and takes his due place in it.

Institutions, then, are organized modes of action, on the basis of the wants and interests which unite men. They differ as the family from the town, the church from the state, according to the scope and character of the wants from which they spring. They are not bare *facts* like objects of knowledge; they are *practical*, existing for the sake of, and by means of the will—as execution of ideas which have interest. Because they are expressions of common purposes and ideas, they are not merely private will and intelligence, but, in the literal sense, *public* will and reason.

The moral endeavor of man thus takes the form

not of isolated fancies about right and wrong, not of attempts to frame a morality for himself, not of efforts to bring into being some praiseworthy ideal never realized; but the form of sustaining and furthering the moral world of which he is a member. Since the world is one of action, and not of contemplation like the world of knowledge, it can be sustained and furthered only as he makes its ends his own, and identifies himself and his satisfaction with the activities in which other wills find their fulfillment.

This is simply a more concrete rendering of what has already been said about the moral environment (see Sec. 33).

LV.

The Aspects of a Moral Institution. An institution is, as we have seen the expression of unity of desires and ideas; it is general intelligence in action, or common will. As such common will, it is, as respects the merely private or exclusive wants and aims of its members, absolutely *sovereign.* It must aim to control them. It must set before them the common end or ideal and insist upon this as the only real end of individual conduct. The ends so imposed by the public reason are *laws.* But these laws are for the sake of realizing the *common* end, of securing that organized unity of action in which alone the individual can find freedom and fullness of action, or his own satisfaction. Thus the activity of the common will gives freedom, or *rights*, to the various members of the institution.

Every institution, then, has its sovereignty, or authority, and its laws and rights. It is only a false abstraction which makes us conceive of sovereignty, or authority, and of law and of rights as inhering only in some supreme organization, as the national state. The family, the school, the neighborhood group, has its authority as respects its members, imposes its ideals of action, or laws, and confers its respective satisfactions in way of enlarged freedom, or rights. It is true that no one of these institutions is isolated; that each stands in relation with other like and unlike institutions. Each minor institution is a member of some more comprehensive whole, to which it bears the same relation that the individual bears to it. That is to say, *its* sovereignty gives way to the authority of the more comprehensive organization; its laws must be in harmony with the laws which flow from the larger activity; its rights must become aspects of a fuller satisfaction. Only humanity or the organized activity of all the wants, powers and interests common to men, can have absolute sovereignty, law and rights.

But the narrower group has its relations, none

the less, although, in ultimate analysis, they flow from and manifest the wider good, which, as wider, must be controlling. Without such minor local authorities, rights and laws, humanity would be a meaningless abstraction, and its activity wholly empty. There is an authority in the family, and the moral growth of the child consists in identifying the law of his own conduct with the ends aimed at by the institution, and in growing into maturity and freedom of manhood through the rights which are bestowed upon him as such a member. Within its own range this institution is ultimate. But its range is not ultimate; the family, valuable and sacred as it is, does not exist for itself. It is not a larger selfishness. It exists as one mode of realizing that comprehensive common good to which all institutions must contribute, if they are not to decay. It is the same with property, the school, the local church, and with the national state.

We can now translate into more concrete terms what was said, in Part I, regarding the good, obligation and freedom. That performance of function which is 'the good', is now seen to consist in vital union with, and reproduction of, the practical institutions of which one is a member. The maintenance of such institutions by the free participation therein of individual wills, is, of itself, the common good. Freedom also gets concreteness; it is the assured rights, or powers of action which one gets as such a member:—powers which are not mere claims, nor simply claims recognized as valid by others, but claims re-inforced by the will of the whole community. Freedom becomes real in the ethical world; it becomes force and efficiency of action, because it does not mean some private possession of the individual, but means the whole coöperating and organized action of an institution in securing to an individual some power of self-expression.

LVI.

Moral Law and the Ethical World. Without the idea of the ethical world, as the unified activity of diverse functions exercised by different individuals, the idea of the good, and of freedom, would be undefined. But probably no one has ever attempted to conceive of the good and of freedom in total abstraction from the normal activity of man. Such has not been the lot of duty, or of the element of law. Often by implication, sometimes in so many words, it is stated that while a physical law may be accounted for, since it is simply an abstract from observed facts, a moral law stands wholly above and apart from actual facts; it expresses solely what 'ought to be' and not what is; that, indeed, whether anything in accordance with it ever has existed or not, is a matter of no essential moral importance theoretically, however it may be practically. Now it is evident that a law of something which has not existed, does not and perhaps never will exist, is essentially inexplicable and mysterious. It is as against such a notion of moral law that the idea of a real ethical world has perhaps its greatest service.

A moral law, *e. g.*, the law of justice, is no more *merely* a law of what ought to be than is the law of gravitation. As the latter states a certain relation of moving masses to one another, so the law of justice states a certain relation of active wills to one another. For a given individual, at a given time and circumstances, the law of justice may appear as the law of something which ought to be, but is not:—is not *for him in this respect*, that is to say. But the very fact that it ought to be for him implies that it already is for others. It *is* a law of the society of which he is a member. And it is because he *is* a member of a society having this law, that is a law of what *should* be for him.

Would then justice cease to be a law for him if it were not observed at all in the society of which he is a member? Such a question is as contradictory as asking what would happen to a planet if the solar system went out of existence. It is the law of justice (with other such laws) that *makes* society; that is, it is those active relations which find expression in these laws that unify individuals so that they have a common end, and thus mutual duties. To imagine the abolition of these laws is to imagine the abolition of society; and to ask for the law of individual conduct apart from all relationship, actual or ideal, to society, is to ask in what morality consists when moral conditions are destroyed. A society in which the social bond we call justice does not obtain to some degree in the relations of man to man, is *not* society; and, on the other hand, wherever some law of justice actually obtains, there the law *is* for every individual who is a member of the society.

This does not mean that the 'is', the actual status of the moral world, is identical with the 'ought', or the ideal relations of man to man. But it does mean that there is no obligation, either in general or as any specific duty, which does not *grow* out of the 'is', the actual relations now obtaining. * The ethical world at any given time is undoubtedly imperfect, and, *therefore*, it demands a certain act to meet the situation. The very imperfection, the very badness in the present condition of things, is a part of the environment with reference to which we must act; it is, thus, an ele-

---

*See Secs. 59, 60 and 63 for discussion of other aspects of this question.

ment in the *law* of future action that it shall not exactly repeat the existing condition. In other words, the 'is' gives the law of the 'ought', but it is a part of this law that the 'ought' shall not be as the 'is'. It is because the relation of justice does hold in members of a stratum of society, having a certain position, power or wealth, but does not hold between this section and another class, that the law of what should be is equal justice for all. In holding that actual social relations afford the law of what should be, we must not forget that these actual relations have a negative as well as a positive side, and that the new law must be framed in view of the negatives, the deficiencies, the wrongs, the contradictions, as well as of the positive attainments. A moral law, to sum up, is the principle of action, which, acted upon, will meet the needs of the existing situation as respects the wants, powers, and circumstances of the individuals concerned. It is no far-away abstraction, but expresses the *movement* of the ethical world.

One example will help define the discussion. Take the case of a street railway conductor, whose union has ordered a strike. What determines the law of his conduct under the circumstances? Evidently the existing ethical institutions of which he is a member, so far as he is conscious of their needs. To determine what he should do, he does not hunt up some law of an 'ought' apart from what is; if he should hunt for and should find such a law he would not know what to do with it. Just because it is apart from his concrete circumstances it is no guide, no law for his conduct at all. He has to act not in view of some abstract principle, but in view of a concrete situation. He considers his present wage, its relation to its needs and abilities; his capacity and taste for this and for that work; the reasons for the strike; the conditions of labor at present with reference to winning the strike, and as to the chance of getting other work. He considers his family, their needs and developing powers; the demand that they should live decently; that his children should be fairly educated and get a fair start in the world; he considers his relationships to his fellow members in the union, etc. These considerations, and such as these, give the law to his decision in so far as he acts morally and not instinctively. Where in this law-giving is there any separation from facts? On the contrary, the more right the act (the nearer it comes to its proper law), the more it will simply express and reflect the actual concrete facts. The law, in other words, of action, is the law of actual social forces in their onward movement, in so far as these demand some response in the way of conduct from the individual.

We may restate from this point of view, what we have already learned: A moral law is thoroughly individualized. It cannot be duplicated; it cannot be for one act just what it is for another. The ethical world is too rich in capacity and circumstance to permit of monotony; it is too swift in its movement to allow of bare repetition. It will not hold still; it moves on, and moral law is the law of action required from individuals by this movement.

The consideration of specific institutions, as the family, industrial society, civil society, the nation, etc., with their respective rights and laws, belongs rather to political philosophy than to the general theory of ethics.

PART III.

THE MORAL LIFE OF THE INDIVIDUAL.

LVII.

Division of Subject. We have now analyzed the fundamental moral notions—the good, duty and freedom; we have considered their objective realization, and seen that they are outwardly expressed in social relations, the more typical and abiding of which we call institutions; that abstract duties are realized in the laws created and imposed by such institutions, and that abstract freedom is realized in the rights possessed by members in them. We have now to consider the concrete moral life of an individual born into this existing ethical world and finding himself confronted with institutions in which he must execute his part, and in which he obtains his satisfaction and free activity. We have to consider how these institutions appeal to the individual, awakening in him a distinct *moral* consciousness, or the consciousness of active relations to persons, in antithesis to the theoretical consciousness of relations which exist in contemplation; how the individual behaves towards these institutions, realizing them by assuming his proper position in them, or attempting to thwart them by living in isolation from them; and how a moral character is thus called into being. More shortly, we have to deal (I) with the practical consciousness, or the formation and growth of ideals of conduct; (II) with the moral struggle, or the process of realizing ideals, and (III) with moral character, or the virtues.

Chapter I.—THE FORMATION AND GROWTH OF IDEALS.

LVIII.

Analysis of Conscience. The practical consciousness, or the recognition of ends and relations of action, is what is usually termed *conscience.* The analysis of conscience shows that it involves three elements, which may be distinguished in theory, although they have no separate existence in the actual fact of conscience itself. These three elements are (1) the knowledge of certain specific forms of conduct, (2) the recognition of the authority or obligatoriness of the forms, and (3) the emotional factors which cluster about this recognition. That is to say, we often speak (1) of conscience telling or informing us of duties; we speak of an enlightened or unenlightened conscience; of savage, or mediæval, or modern conscience. Here we are evidently thinking of the kind and range of particular acts considered right or wrong. But we also speak (2) of the authority and majesty of conscience; of the commands of conscience, etc. Here we are thinking of the consciousness of *obligation in general.* The savage and the civilized man may vary greatly in their estimate of what particular acts are right or wrong, and yet agree in the recognition that such acts as are right are absolutely obligatory. Finally we speak of an approving or disapproving, or remorseful conscience, of a tender or a hardened conscience, of the pangs, the pricks of conscience, etc. Here (3) we are evidently dealing with the responsiveness of the disposition to moral distinctions, either in particular acts, or in the recognition of moral law in general.

LVIX.

Conscience as the Recognition of Special Acts as Right or Wrong.

Conscience in this sense is no peculiar, separate faculty of mind. It is simply intelligence dealing with a certain subject-matter. That is, conscience is distinguished not by the kind of mental activity at work, but by the kind of material the mind works upon. Intelligence deals with the nature and relations of things, and we call it understanding; intelligence deals with the relations of persons and deeds, and it is termed conscience.

We may, with advantage, recognize these stages in the development of intelligence as dealing with moral relationships:

1. *The Customary or Conventional Conscience.* The existing moral world, with the types and varieties of institutions peculiar to it, is constantly impressing itself upon the immature mind; it makes certain demands of moral agents and enforces them with all the means in its power—punishment, reward, blame, public-opinion, and the bestowal of social leadership. These demands and expectations naturally give rise to certain convictions in the individual as to what he should or should not do. Such convictions are not the outcome of independent reflection, but of the moulding influence of social institutions. Moreover the morality of a time becomes consolidated into proverbs, maxims and law-codes. It takes shape in certain habitual ways of looking at and judging matters. All these are instilled into the growing mind through language, literature, association and legal custom, until they leave in the mind a corresponding habit and attitude toward things to be done. This process may be compared to the proc-

ess by which knowledge of the world of things is first attained. Certain of the more permanent features of this world, especially those whose observance is important in relation to continued physical existence and well-being, impress themselves upon the mind. Consciousness, with no reflective activity of its own, comes to mirror some of the main outlines of the world. The more important distinctions are fixed in language, and they find their way into the individual mind, giving it unconsciously a certain bent and coloring.

2. *The Loyal Conscience.* But just as the mind, which seems at first to have the facts and features of the world poured into itself as a passive vessel, comes in time through its own experience to appreciate something of their meaning, and, to some extent, to verify them for itself; so the mind in its moral relations. Without forming any critical theory of the institutions and codes which are forming character, without even considering whether they are what they should be, the individual yet comes at least to a practical recognition that it is in these institutions that he gets his satisfactions, and through these codes that he is protected. He identifies himself, his own life, with the social forms and ideals in which he lives, and repels any attack upon them as he would an attack

upon himself. The demands which the existing institutions make upon him are not felt as the coercions of a despot, but as expressions of his own will, and requiring loyalty as such. The conventional conscience, if it does not grow into this, tends to become slavish, while an intelligence which practically realizes, although without continual reflection, the *significance* of conventional morality is *free* in its convictions and service.

3. *The Independent or Reflective Conscience.* The intelligence may not simply appropriate, as its own, conventions embodied in current institutions and codes, but may *reflect* upon them. It may ask: What is this institution of family, property for? Does the institution in its present form work as it should work, or is some modification required? Does this rule which is now current embody the true needs of the situation, or is it an antiquated expression of by-gone relations? What is the true spirit of existing institutions, and what sort of conduct does this spirit demand?

Here, in a word, we have the same relation to the ethical world, that we have in physical science to the external world. Intelligence is not content, on its theoretical side, with having facts impressed upon it by direct contact or through language; it is not content with coming to feel for itself the value of the truths so impressed. It assumes an independent attitude, putting itself over against nature and cross-questioning her. It proposes its own ideas, its own theories and hypotheses, and manipulates facts to see if this rational meaning can be verified. It criticises what passes as truth, and pushes on to more adequate statement.

The correlative attempt, on the part of intelligence on its practical side, may have a larger or a smaller scope. In its wider course it aims to criticise and to re-form prevailing social ideals and institutions — even those apparently most fixed. This is the work of the great moral teachers of the world. But in order that conscience be critical, it is not necessary that its range be so wide. The average member of a civilized community is nowadays called upon to reflect upon his immediate relationships in life, to see if they are what they should be; to regulate his own conduct by rules which he follows not simply because they are customary, but the result of his own examination of the situation. There is no difference in kind between the grander and the minuter work. And it is only the constant exercise of reflective examination on the smaller scale which makes possible, and which gives efficiency to, the deeper criticism and transformation.

LX.

Reflective Conscience and the Ethical World. This conception of conscience as critical and reflective is one of the chief fruits of the Socratic ethics, fructified by the new meaning given life through the Christian spirit. It involves the 'right of free conscience'—the right of the individual to know the good, to know the end of action, for himself, rather than to have some good, however imposing and however beneficent, enjoined from without. It is this principle of subjective freedom, says Hegel, which marks the turning-point in the distinction of modern from ancient times (Sec. 124, *Grundlinien der Philosophie des Rechts*, Vol. VIII of Hegel's Works).*

But this notion of conscience is misinterpreted when the content as well as the form of conscience is thought to be individual. There is no right of private judgment, in the sense that there is not a public source and standard of judgment. What is meant by this right is that the standard, the source, is not the opinion of some other person, or group of persons. It is a common, objective standard. It is that embodied in social relationships themselves.

---

*I hardly need say how largely I am indebted in the treatment of this topic, and indeed, in the whole matter of the 'ethical world', to Hegel.

The conception of conscience as a private possession, to be exercised by each one in independence of historical forms and contemporary ideals, is thoroughly misleading. The saying "I had to follow my own notion of what is right" has been made the excuse for all sorts of capricious, obstinate and sentimental performance. It is of such notions that Hegel further says: "The striving for a morality of one's own is futile, and by its very nature impossible of attainment; in respect of morality the saying of the wisest men of antiquity is the only true one: To be moral is to live in accordance with the moral tradition of one's country" (Hegel, Works, Vol. I, p. 389). And in discussing the same question, Bradley has said that the wish to have a morality of one's own better than that of the world is to be on the threshold of morality (p. 180).

Yet, on the other hand, conscience should not simply repeat the burden of existing usages and opinions. No one can claim that the existing morality embodies the highest possible conception of personal relations. A morality which does not recognize both the possibility and the necessity of advance is immorality. Where then is the way out from a capricious self-conceit, on one hand, and a dead conformity on the other? Reflective conscience must be *based* on the moral consciousness expressed in existing institutions, manners and beliefs. Otherwise it is empty and arbitrary. But the existing moral status is never wholly self-consistent. It realizes ideals in one relation which it does not in another; it gives rights to 'aristocrats' which it denies to low-born; to men, which it refuses to women; it exempts the rich from obligations which it imposes upon the poor. Its institutions embody a common good which turns out to be good only to a privileged few, and thus existing in self-contradiction. They suggest ends which they execute only feebly or intermittently. Reflective intelligence cross-questions the existing morality; and extracts from it the ideal which it pretends to embody, and thus is able to criticise the existing morality in the light of its *own* ideal. It points out the inconsistencies, the incoherencies, the compromises, the failures, between the actual practice and the theory at the basis of this practice. And thus the new ideal proposed by the individual is not a product of his private opinions, but is the outcome of the ideal embodied in existing customs, ideas and institutions.

LXI.

The Sense of Obligation. There has been much discussion regarding the nature of the act of mind by which obligation is recognized. A not uncommon view has been that the sense of duty as such must be the work of a peculiar faculty of the mind. Admitting that the recognition of this or that particular thing as right or wrong, is the work of ordinary intelligence, it is held that the additional recognition of the absolute obligatoriness of the right cannot be the work of this intelligence. For our intellect is confined to judging what is or has been; the conception of obligation, of something which should be, wholly transcends its scope. There is, therefore, some special moral in faculty called which affixes to the ordinary judgments the stamp of the categorical imperative "You ought".

See for example Maurice on "Conscience". The view is traceable historically to Kant's conception of Practical Reason, but as the view is ordinarily advanced the function of Practical Reason in Kant's philosophy is overlooked. The Practical Reason is no special faculty of man's being; it is his consciousness of himself as an acting being; that is, as a being capable of acting from ideas. Kant never separates the consciousness of duty from the very nature of will as the realization of conceptions. In the average modern presentation, this intrinsic connection of duty with activity is absent. Conscience becomes a faculty whose function it is to clap the idea of duty upon the existent conception of an act; and this existent conception is regarded as morally indifferent.

It is true that Kant's Practical Reason has a certain separateness or isolation. But this is because of his general separation of the rational from the sensuous factor, and not because of any separation of the consciousness of action from the consciousness of duty. If Kant erred in his divorce of desire and duty, then even the relative apartness of the Practical Reason must be given up. The consciousness of obligation is involved in the recognition of *any* end of conduct, and not simply in the end of abstract law.

Such a conception of conscience, however, is open to serious objections. Aside from the fact that large numbers of men declare that no amount of introspection reveals any such machinery within themselves, this separate faculty seems quite superflous. The real distinction is not between the consciousness of an action with, and without, the recognition of duty, but between a consciousness which is and one which is not capable of conduct. Any being who is capable of putting before himself ideas as motives of conduct, who is capable of forming a conception of something which he would realize, is, by that very fact, capable of a sense of obligation. The consciousness of an end to be realized, the idea of something to be done, is, in and of itself, the consciousness of duty.

Let us consider again the horse-car conductor (see Sec. LVI). After he has analyzed the situation which faces him and decided that a given course of conduct is the one which fits the situation, does he require some additional faculty to inform him that this course is the one which should be followed? The analysis of practical ideas, that is, of proposed ends of conduct, is from the first an analysis of what should be done. Such being the case, it is no marvel that the conclusion of the reflection is: "This should (ought to) be done."

Indeed, just as every judgment about existent fact naturally takes the form 'S *is* P', so every judgment regarding an activity which executes an idea takes the form, 'S ought (or ought not) to be P'. It requires no additional faculty of mind, after intelligence has been studying the motions of the moon, to insert itself, and affirm some objective relation or truth—as that the moon's motions are explainable by the law of gravitation. It is the very essence of theoretical judgment, judgment regarding fact, to state truth—what is. And it is the very essence of practical judgment, judgment regarding deeds, to state that active relation which we call obligation, what *ought to be.*

The judgment as to what a practical situation *is*, is an untrue or abstract judgment.

The practical situation is itself an *activity*; the needs, powers, and circumstances which make it are moving on. At no instant in time is the scene quiescent. But the agent, in order to determine his course of action in view of this situation, has to *fix* it; he has to arrest its onward movement in order to tell what it is. So his abstracting intellect cuts a cross-section through its on-going, and says 'This *is* the situation'. Now the judgment 'This ought to be the situation', or 'in view of the situation, my conduct ought to be thus and so', is simply restoring the movement which the mind has temporarily put out of sight. By means of its cross-section, intelligence has detected the principle, or law of movement, of the situation, and it is on the basis of this movement that conscience declares what ought to be.

Just as the fact of moral law, or of authority, of the incumbency of duty, needs for its explanation no separation of the 'is' from the 'ought' (see LVI), but only recognition of the law of the 'is' which is, perforce, a law of movement, and of change;—so the consciousness of law, 'the sense of obligation' requires no special mental faculty which may declare what ought to be. The intelligence that is capable of declaring truth, or what is, is capable also of making known obligation. For obligation is only *practical* truth, the 'is' of doing.

See upon this point, as well as upon the relation of laws and rules to action, my article in Vol. I, No. 2, of the International Journal of Ethics, entitled 'Moral Theory and Practice'.

LXII.

Conscience as Emotional Disposition. Probably no judgment is entirely free from emotional coloring and accompaniments. It is doubtful whether the most indifferent judgment is not based upon, and does not appeal to, some interest. Certainly all the more important judgments awaken some response from the self, and excite its interests to their depths. Some of them may be excited by the intrinsic nature of the subject-matter under judgment, while others are the results of associations more or less accidental. The former will necessarily be aroused in every being, who has any emotional nature at all, whenever the judgment is made, while the latter will vary from time to time, and may entirely pass away. That moral judgments, judgments of what should be (or should have been) done, arouse emotional response, is therefore no cause for surprise. It may help clear up difficulties if we distinguish three kinds of such emotional accompaniment.

1. There are, first, the interests belonging to the sense of obligation as such. We have just seen that this sense of obligation is nothing separate from the consciousness of the particular act which is to be performed. Nevertheless the consciousness of obligation, of an authority and law, recurs with every act, while the special content of the act constantly varies. Thus an idea of law, or of duty in general, is formed, distinct from any special duty. Being formed, it arouses the special emotional excitation appropriate to it. The formation of this general idea of duty, and the growth of

feeling of duty as such, is helped on through the fact that children (and adults so far as their moral life is immature) need to have their moral judgments constantly reinforced by recurrence to the thought of law. That is to say, a child, who is not capable of seeing the true moral bearings and claims of an act, is yet continually required to perform such an act on the ground that it *is* obligatory. The feeling, therefore, is natural and legitimate. It must, however, go hand in hand with the feelings aroused by the special moral relations under consideration. Disconnected from such union, it necessarily leads to slavish and arbitrary forms of conduct. A child, for example, who is constantly taught to perform acts simply because he *ought* to do so, without having at the same time his intelligence directed to the nature of the act which is obligatory (without, that is, being led to see how or why it is obligatory), may have a strongly developed sense of obligation. As he grows up, however, this sense of duty will be largely one of dread and apprehension; a feeling of constraint, rather than of free service. Besides this, it will be largely a matter of accident to what act this feeling attaches itself. Anything that comes to the mind with the force of associations of past education, any ideal that forces itself persistently into consciousness from any source may awaken this sense of obligation, wholly irrespective of the true nature of the act. This is the explanation of strongly 'conscientious' persons, whose morality is yet unintelligent and blundering. It is of such persons that it has been said that a thoroughly *good* man can do more harm than a number of bad men.

When, however, the feeling of obligation in general is developed along with particular moral judgments (that is, along with the habit of considering the special nature of acts performed), it is one of the strongest supports to morality. Acts constantly need to be performed which are recognized as right and as obligatory, and yet with reference to which there is no fixed habit of conduct. In these cases, the more direct, or spontaneous, stimulus to action is wanting.

If, however, there is a strong sense of obligation in general, this may attach itself to the particular act and thus afford the needed impetus. In unusual experiences, and in cases where the ordinary motive-forces are lacking, such a feeling of regard for law may be the only sure stay of right conduct.

2. There is the emotional accompaniment appropriate to the special content of the act. If, for example, the required act has to do with some person, there arise in consciousness the feelings of

interest, of love and friendship, or of dislike, which belong to that person. If it relate to some piece of work to be done, the sweeping of a room, the taking of a journey, the painting of a picture, there are the interests natural to such subjects. These feelings when aroused necessarily form part of the emotional attitude as respects the act. It is the strength and normal welling-up of such specific interests which afford the best assurance of healthy and progressive moral conduct, as distinct from mere sentimental dwelling upon ideals. Only interests prevent the divorce of feelings and ideas from habits of action. Such interests are the union of the subjective element, the self, and the objective, the special relations to be realized (Sec. XXXIV), and thus necessarily produce a right and healthy attitude towards moral ends. It is obvious that in a normal moral life, the law of obligation in general, and the specific interests in particular cases, should more and more fuse. The interests, at their strongest, take the form of *love.* And thus there is realized the ideal of an effective character; the union of law and inclination in its pure form — love for the action in and of itself.

3. Emotions due to accidental associations. It is matter of common notice that the moral feelings are rarely wholly pure; that all sorts of sentiments,

due to associations of time and place and person not strictly belonging to the acts themselves, cluster about them. While this is true, we should not forget the great difficulty there is in marking off any associations as *wholly* external to the nature of the act. We may say that mere fear of punishment is such a wholly external feeling, having no place in moral emotion. Yet it may be doubted whether there is any feeling that may be called mere fear of punishment. It is, perhaps, fear of punishment by a parent, for whom one has love and respect, and thus the fear has partially a genuinely moral aspect. Some writers would call the æsthetic feelings, the feelings of beauty, of harmony, which gather about moral ends adventitious. Yet the fact that other moralists have made all moral feelings essentially æsthetic, as due to the perception of the fitness and proportion of the acts, should warn us from regarding æsthetic feelings as wholly external. About all that can be said is that feelings which do not spring from *some* aspect of the content of the act itself should be extruded, with growing maturity of character, from influence upon conduct.

LXIII.

Conscientiousness. Conscientiousness is primarily the virtue of intelligence in regard to conduct. That is to say, it is the formed habit of bringing intelligence to bear upon the analysis of moral relations—the habit of considering what ought to be done. It is based upon the recognition of the idea first distinctly formulated by Socrates—that "an unexamined life is not one that should be led by man". It is the outgrowth of the customary morality embodied in usages, codes and social institutions, but it is an advance upon custom, because it requires a meaning and a reason. It is the mark of a "character which will not be satisfied without understanding the law that it obeys; without knowing what the good is, for which the demand has hitherto been blindly at work" (Green, Op. cit., p. 270). Conscientiousness, then, is reflective intelligence grown into character. It involves a greater and wider recognition of obligation in general, and a larger and more stable emotional response to everything that presents itself as duty; as well as the habit of deliberate consideration of the moral situation and of the acts demanded by it.

Conscientiousness is an analysis of the conditions under which conduct takes place, and of the action that will meet these conditions; it is a thoroughly *objective* analysis. What is sometimes termed conscientiousness is merely the habit of analyzing internal moods and sentiments; of prying into 'motives' in that sense of motive which identifies it not with the end of action, but with some subjective state of emotion. Thus considered, conscientiousness is morbid. We are sometimes warned against *over*-conscientiousness. But such conscientiousness means simply over-regard of one's private self; keeping an eye upon the effect of conduct on one's internal state, rather than upon conduct itself. Over-conscientiousness is as impossible as over-intelligence, since it is simply the application of intelligence to conduct. It is as little morbid and introspective as is the analysis of any fact in nature. Another notion which is sometimes thought to be bound up with that of conscience, also has nothing to do with it; namely, the notion of a precision and coldness opposed to all large spontaneity and broad sympathy in conduct. The reflective man of narrow insight and cramped conduct is often called the conscientious man and opposed to the man of generous impulses. This comes from identifying conscience with a ready-made code of rules, and its action with the application of some such fixed code to all acts as they come up. It is evident, on the contrary, that such a habit is opposed to conscience. Conscience means the consideration of each case *in itself;* measuring it not by any outside code, but in the existing moral situation.

On conscientiousness, see Green, Op. cit., pp. 269-271 and 323-327; and Alexander, Op. cit., pp. 156-160. These writers, however, seem to identify it too much with internal scrutiny. Green, for example, expressly identifies conscientiousness with a man's "questioning about himself, whether he has been as good as he should have been, whether a better man would not have acted otherwise than he has done" (p. 323). He again speaks of it as "comparison of our own practice, as we know it on the inner side in relation to the motives and character which it expresses, with an ideal of virtue". The first definition seems to be misleading. Questioning as to whether the end adopted was what it should have been, *i. e.*, whether the analysis of the situation was correctly performed, may be of great service in aiding future decisions, but questioning regarding the purity of one's own 'motive' does not seem of much avail. In a man upon the whole good, such questioning is apt to be paralyzing. The energy that should go to conduct goes to anxiety about one's conduct. It is the view of goodness as directed mainly towards one's own private motives, which has led such writers as Henry James, Sr., and Mr. Hinton, to conceive of 'morality', the struggle for goodness, to be in essence bad. They conceived of the struggle for 'private goodness' as no different from the struggle for private pleasure, although likely, of course, to lead to better things. Nor in a bad man is such scrutiny of 'motive', as apart from objective end, of much value. The bad man is generally aware of the badness of his motive without much close examination. The truth aimed at by Green is, I think, amply covered by recognizing that conscientiousness as a constant will to know what should be, and to readjust conduct to meet the new insight, is the spring of the moral life.

LXIV.

Moral Commands, Rules and Systems. What is the part played by specific commands and by general rules in the examination of conduct by conscience? We should note, in the first place, that commands are not rules, and rules are not commands. A command, to be a command, must be specific and individual. It must refer to time, place and circumstance. 'Thou shalt do no murder' is not strictly speaking a command, for it allows questioning as to what is murder. Is killing in war murder? Is the hanging of criminals murder? Is taking life in self-defense murder? Regarded simply as a command, this command would be 'void for uncertainty'. A true command is a specific injunction of one person to another to do or not to do a stated thing or things. Under what conditions do commands play a part in moral conduct? In cases where the intelligence of the agent is so undeveloped that he cannot realize for himself the situation and see the act required, and when a part of the agent's environment is constituted by others who have such required knowledge, there *is* a moral element in command and in obedience.

This explains the moral responsibility of parents to children and of children to parents. The soldier, too, in recognizing a general's command, is recognizing the situation as it exists for him. Were there simply superior force on one side, and fear on the other, the relation would be an immoral one. It is implied, of course, in such an instance as the parents' command, that it be so directed as to enable the child more and more to dispense with it—that is, that it be of such a character as to give the child insight into the situation for himself. Here is the transition from a command to a rule.

A rule does not tell what to do or what to leave undone. The Golden Rule, for example, does not tell me how to act in any specific case. *A rule is a tool of analysis.* The moral situation, or capacity in its relation to environment, is often an extremely complicated affair. How shall the individual resolve it? How shall he pick it to pieces, so as to see its real nature and the act demanded by it? It is evident that the analysis will be the more truly and speedily performed if the agent has a method by which to attack it, certain principles in the light of which he may view it, instruments for cross-questioning it and making it render up its meaning. Moral rules perform this service. While the Golden Rule does not of itself give one jot of information as to what I should do in a given case, it does, if accepted, immensely simplify the situation. Without it I should perhaps have to act blindly; with it the question comes to this: What should I, under the given circumstances, like to have done to me? This settled, the whole question of what should be done is settled.

It is obvious, then, that the value of a moral rule depends upon its potency in revealing the inner spirit and reality of individual deeds. Rules in the negative form, rules whose application is limited in scope because of an attempt to be specific, are midway between commands proper and rules. The Golden Rule, on the other hand, is positive, and not attempting to define any specific act, covers in its range all relations of man to man. It is indeed only a concrete and forcible statement of the ethical principle itself, the idea of a common good, or of a community of persons. This is also a convenient place for considering the practical value of ethical systems. We have already seen that no system can attempt to tell what in particular should be done. The principle of a system, however, may be of some aid in analyzing a specific case. In this way, a system may be regarded as a highly generalized rule. It attempts to state some fundamental principle which lies at the basis of moral conduct. So far as it succeeds in doing this, there is the possibility of its practical application in particular cases, although, of course, the mediate rules must continue to be the working tools of mankind—on account of their decided concrete character, and because they have themselves taken shape under the pressure of practice rather than of more theoretical needs.

LXV.

Development of Moral Ideals. Thus far we have been speaking of conscience mainly as to its method of working. We have now to speak more definitely of its content, or of the development of ideals of action.

It is of the very nature of moral conduct to be progressive. Permanence of *specific* ideals means moral death. We say that truth-telling, charity, loyalty, temperance, have always been moral ends; and while this is true, the statement as ordinarily made is apt to hide from us the fact that the content of the various ideals (what is *meant* by temperance, etc.) has been constantly changing, and this of necessity. The realization of moral ends must bring about a changed situation, so that the repetition of the same ends would no longer satisfy. This progress has two sides: the satisfaction of wants leads to a larger view of what satisfaction really is, *i. e.*, to the creation of new capacities and wants; while adjustment to the environment creates wider and more complex social relationships.

Let the act be one of intelligence. Some new fact or law is discovered. On one hand, this discovery may arouse a hitherto comparatively dormant mind; it may suggest the possession of capacities previously latent; it may stimulate mental activity and create a thirst for expanding knowledge. This readjustment of intellectual needs and powers may be comparatively slight, or it may amount, as it has with many a young person, to a revolution. On the other hand, the new fact changes the intellectual outlook, the mental horizon, and, by transforming somewhat the relations of things, demands new conduct. All this, even when the growth of knowledge concerns only the physical world. But development of insight into social needs and affairs has a larger and more direct progressive influence. The social world exists spiritually, as conceived, and a new conception of it, new perception of its scope and bearings, is, perforce, a change of that world. And thus it is with the satisfaction of the human want of knowledge, that patience, courage, self-respect, humility, benevolence, all change character. When, for example, psychology has given an increase of knowledge regarding men's motives, political economy an increase of knowledge regarding men's wants, when historical knowledge has added its testimony regarding the effects of indiscriminate giving, charity must change its content. While once, the mere supplying of food or money by one to another may have been right as meeting the recognized relations, charity now comes to mean large responsibility in knowledge of antecedents and circumstances, need of organization, careful tracing of consequences, and, above all, effort to remove the conditions which made the want possible. The activity involved has infinitely widened.

Let the act be in the region of industrial life—a new invention. The invention of the telephone does not simply satisfy an old want—it creates new. It brings about the possibility of closer social relations, extends the distribution of intelligence, facilitates commerce. It is a common saying that the luxury of one generation is the necessity of the next; that is to say, what once satisfied a somewhat remote need becomes in time the basis upon which new needs grow up. Energy previously pent up is set free, new power and ideals are evoked. Consider again a person assuming a family relation. This seems, at first, to consist mainly in the satisfaction of certain common and obvious human wants. But this satisfaction, if moral, turns out rather to be the creation of new insight into life, of new relationships, and thus of new energies and ideals. We may generalize these instances. The secret of the moral life is not getting or having, it is doing and thus being. The getting and the possessing side of life has a moral value only when it is made the stimulus and nutriment of new and wider acting. To solve the equation between getting and doing is the moral problem of life. Let the possession be acquiesced in for its own sake, and not as the way to freer (and thus more moral) action, and the selfish life has set in (see Sec. LXVII). It is essential to moral activity that it feed itself into larger appetites and thus into larger life.

This must not be taken to deny that there is a mechanical side even to the moral life. A merchant, for example, may do the same thing over and over again, like going to his business every morning at the same hour. This is a moral act and yet it does not seem to lead to a change in moral wants or surroundings. Yet even in such cases it should be noted that it is only outwardly that the act is the *same*. In itself, that is, in its relation to the will of the agent, it is simply one element in the whole of character; and as character opens up, the act must change somewhat also. It is performed somehow in a new spirit. If this is not to some extent true, if such acts become wholly mechanical, the moral life is hardening into the rigidity of death.

This progressive development consists on one side in a richer and subtler individual activity, in increased individualization, in wider and freer functions of life; on the other it consists in increase in number of those persons whose ideal is a 'common good', or who have membership in the same moral community; and, further, it consists in more complex relations between them. It is both intensive and extensive.

History is one record of growth in the sense of specific powers. Its track is marked by the appearance of more and more internal and distinguishing traits; of new divisions of labor and corresponding freedom in functioning. It begins with groups in which everything is massed, and the good is common only in the sense of being undifferentiated for all. It progresses with the evolution of individuality, of the peculiar gifts entrusted to each, and hence of the specific service demanded of each.

The other side, the enlargement of the community of ends, has been termed growth in "comprehensiveness". History is again a record of the widening of the social consciousness—of the range of persons whose interests have to be taken into account in action. There has been a period in which the community was nothing more than a man's own immediate family group, this enlarging to the clan, the city, the social class, the nation; until now, in theory, the community of interests and ends is humanity itself.

This growth in comprehensiveness is not simply a growth in the number of persons having a common end. The quantitative growth reacts upon the *nature* of the ends themselves. For example, when the conceived community is small, bravery may consist mainly in willingness to fight for the recognized community against other hostile groups. As these groups become themselves included in the moral community, courage must change its form, and become resoluteness and integrity of purpose in defending manhood and humanity as such. That is to say, as long as the community is based largely upon physical facts, like oneness of blood, of territory, etc., the ideal of courage will have a somewhat external and physical manifestation. Let the community be truly spiritual, consisting in recognition of unity of destiny and function in coöperation toward an all-inclusive life, and the ideal of courage becomes more internal and spiritual, consisting in loyalty to the possibilities of humanity, whenever and wherever found.

On this development of moral ideals, and especially of the growth in "comprehensiveness" as reacting upon the intrinsic form which the ideal itself takes, see Green, Op. cit., pp. 264–308, followed by Alexander, Op. cit., pp. 384–398. For the process of change of ideals in general, see Alexander, pp. 271–292, and 369–371.

Chapter II.—THE MORAL STRUGGLE OR THE REALIZING OF IDEALS.

LXVI.

Goodness as a Struggle. We have already seen that the bare repetition of identically the same acts does not consist with morality. To aim at securing a satisfaction precisely like the one already experienced, is to fail to recognize the altered capacity and environment, and the altered duty. Moral satisfaction prior to an act is *ideal;* ideal not simply in the sense of being conceived, or present to thought, but ideal in the sense that it has not been already enjoyed. Some satisfaction has been enjoyed in a previous activity, but that very satisfaction has so enlarged and complicated the situation, that its mere repetition would not afford moral or active satisfaction, but only what Kant terms 'pathological' satisfaction. Morality thus assumes the form of a struggle. The past satisfaction speaks for itself; it has been verified in experience, it has conveyed its worth to our very senses. We have tried and tasted it, and know that it is good. If morality lay in the repetition of similar satisfactions, it would not be a struggle. We should know experimentally before hand that the chosen end would bring us satisfaction, and should be at rest in that knowledge. But when morality lies in striving for satisfactions which have not verified themselves to our sense, it always requires an effort. We have to surrender the enjoyed good, and stake ourselves upon that of which we cannot say: We *know* it is good. To surrender the actual experienced good for a possible ideal good is the struggle.

We arrive, in what is termed the opposition of desire and duty, at the heart of the moral struggle. Of course, taken strictly, there can be no opposition here. The duty which did not awaken *any* desire would not appeal to the mind even as a duty. But we may distinguish between a desire which is based on past satisfaction actually experienced, and desire based simply upon the idea that the end is *desirable*—that it ought to be desired. It may seem strange to speak of a desire based simply upon the recognition that an end *should* be desired, but the possibility of awakening such a desire and the degree of its strength are the test of a moral character. How far does this end awaken response in me because I see that it is the end which is fit and due? How far does it awaken this response although it does not fall into line with past satisfactions, or although it actually thwart some habitual satisfaction? Here is the opposition of duty and desire. It lies in the contrast of a good which has demonstrated itself as such in experience, and a good whose claim to be good rests only on the fact that it is the act which meets the situation. It is the contrast between a good of possession, and one of action.

From this point of view morality is a life of *aspiration*, and of *faith;* there is required constant willingness to give up past goods as the good, and to press on to new ends; not because past achievements are bad, but because, being good, they have created a situation which demands larger and more intricately related achievements. This willingness is aspiration and it implies *faith.* ' Only the old good is of sight, has verified itself to sense. The new ideal, the end which meets the situation, is felt as good only in so far as the character has formed the conviction that to meet obligation is itself a good, whether bringing sensible satisfaction or not. You can prove to a man that he ought to act so and so (that is to say, that such an act is the one which fits the present occasion), but you cannot *prove* to him that the performance of that duty will be good. Only faith in the moral order, in the identity of duty and the good, can assert this. Every time an agent takes as his end (that is, chooses as good) an activity which he has not already tried, he asserts his belief in the goodness of right action as such. This faith is not a mere intellectual thing, but it is practical—the staking of self upon activity as against passive possession.

LXVII.

Moral Badness. Badness originates in the contrast which thus comes about between *having* the repetition of former action, and *doing*—pressing forward to the new right action. Goodness is the choice of doing; the refusal to be content with past good as exhausting the entire content of goodness. It is, says Green, 'in the continued effort to be better that goodness consists'. The man, however bad his past and however limited his range of intellectual, æsthetic and social activity, who is dissatisfied with his past, and whose dissatisfaction manifests itself in act, is accounted better than the man of a respectable past and higher plane of life who has lapsed into contented acquiescence with past deeds. For past deeds are not *deeds*, they are passive enjoyments. The bad man, on the other hand, is not the man who loves badness *in and for itself*. Such a man would be a mad man or a devil. All conduct, bad as well as good, is for the sake of *some* satisfaction, that is, some good. In the bad man, the satisfaction which is aimed at is *simply* the one congruent with existing inclinations, irrespective of the sufficiency of those inclinations in view of the changed capacity and environment: it is a good of *having*. The bad man, that is to say, does not recognize any *ideal* or *active* good; any good which has not already commended itself to him as such. This good may be good in *itself*; but, as distinguished from the good which requires action, that which would fulfill the present capacity or meet the present situation, it is bad.

Thus Alexander terms badness *a survival*, in part at least, of former goodness. Hinton says (Philosophy and Religion, p. 146), "That a thing is wrong does not mean that it ought never to have been done or thought, but that it ought to be left off". It will be noted that we are not dealing with the metaphysical or the religious problem of the nature and origin of evil, but simply with an account of bad action as it appears in individual conduct.

Badness has four traits, all derivable from this basal fact. They are: (1) Lawlessness, (2) Selfishness, (3) Baseness, (4) Demoralization.

1. *Lawlessness.* When desire and duty, that is, when desires based on past having and on future acting, conflict, the bad man lets duty go. He virtually denies that it is a good at all—it may be a good in the abstract but not a good for him. He denies that obligation as such has any value; that any end is to be consulted save his own state of mind. He denies that there is law for conduct—at least any law beyond the inclination which he happens to have at the time of action. Keeping himself within that which has verified itself to his feeling in the past, he abrogates all authority excepting that of his own immediate feelings.

2. *Selfishness.* It has already been shown that the self is not necessarily immoral, and hence that action for self is not necessarily bad—indeed, that the true self is social and interest in it right (see Sec. XXXV). But when a satisfaction based on

past experience is set against one proceeding from an act as meeting obligation, there grows up a divorce in the self. The actual self, the self recognizing only past and sensible satisfaction, is set over against the self which recognizes the necessity of expansion and a wider environment. Since the former self confines its action to benefits demonstrably accruing to itself, while the latter, in meeting the demands of the situation, necessarily contributes to the satisfaction of others, one takes the form of a *private* self, a self whose good is set over against and exclusive of that of others, while the self recognizing obligation becomes a social self—the self which performs its due function in society. It is, again, the contrast between getting and doing.

All moral action is based upon the presupposition of the identity of good (Sec. XL), but it by no means follows that this identity of good can be demonstrated to the agent at the time of action. On the contrary, it is matter of the commonest experience that the sensible good, the demonstrable good (that is, the one visible on the line of past satisfaction) may be contradictory to the act which would satisfy the interests of others. The identity of interests can be proved *only by acting upon it;* to the agent, prior to action, it is a matter of faith. Choice presents itself then in these cases as a test:

Do you believe that the Good is simply your private good, or is the true Good, is *your* good, one which includes the good of others? The condemnation passed upon the 'selfish' man is that he virtually declares that good is essentially exclusive and private. He shuts himself up within himself, within, that is, his past achievements, and the inclinations based upon them. The good man goes out of himself in new action. Bad action is thus essentially narrowing, it confines the self; good action is expansive and vital, it moves on to a larger self.

In fine, all conduct, good and bad, satisfies the self; bad conduct, however, aims at a self which, keeping its eye upon its private and assured satisfaction, refuses to recognize the increasing function with its larger social range,—the 'selfish' self.

Light is thrown upon this point by referring to what was said about interest (Sec. XXXIV). Interest is *active* feeling, feeling turned upon an object, and going out toward it so as to identify it with self. In this active and objective interest there is satisfaction, but the satisfaction is *in* the activity which has the object for its content. This is the satisfaction of the good self. In the bad self, interest is reduced to mere feeling; for the aim of life in such a self is simply to have certain feelings as its own possession; activity and its object are degraded into mere means for getting these sensations.

Activity has two sides; as activity, as projection or expression of one's powers, it satisfies self; as activity, also, it has some end, some object, for its content. The activity as such, therefore, the activity for its own sake, must involve the realization of this object for its own sake. But in having, in getting, there is no such creation or maintenance of an object for itself. Objects cease to be 'ends in themselves' when they cease to be the content of action; and are degraded into means of private satisfaction, that is, of sensation.

3. *Baseness.* For, when we say that bad action takes account of ideals only on the basis of possession, we say, in effect, that it takes account only of *sensible* satisfaction. As it is in the progressive movement of morality that there arises the distinction of the law-abiding and the lawless self, of the social and the selfish self, so in the same aspect there comes into existence the distinction of the low, degraded, sensual self, as against the higher or spiritual self. In themselves, or naturally, there is no desire high, none low. But when an inclination for an end which consists in possession comes into conflict with one which includes an active satisfaction — one not previously enjoyed — the contrast arises. It is wrong to say, with Kant, that the bad act is simply for pleasure; for the bad act, the choice of a past satisfaction as against the aspira-

tion for a wider good, may have a large content—it may be the good of one's family; it may be scientific or æsthetic culture. Yet the moment a man begins to live on the plane of past satisfaction as such, he has begun to live on the plane of 'sense', or for pleasure. The refusal to recognize the ideal good, to acknowledge activity as good, throws the agent back into a life of dwelling upon his own sensible good, and thus he falls more and more into a life of dwelling upon mere sensations. What made the past good a good at all was the spirit, the activity, in it, and when it is no longer an activity, but a mere keeping, the life is gone out of it. The selfish life must degenerate into mere sensuality—although when sensuality is 'refined' we call it sentimentality.

4. *Demoralization.* Morality is activity; exercise of function. To cease this activity is not to remain on the attained level, for that, *when attained*, was active. It is to relapse, to slip down into badness. The moral end is always an activity. To fail in this activity is, therefore, to involve character in disintegration. It can be kept together only by constant organizing activity; only by acting upon new wants and moving toward new situations. Let this activity cease, and disorganization ensues, as surely as the body decays when life goes, instead of simply remaining inert as it was. Bad conduct

is thus *unprincipled;* it has no center, no movement. The good man is 'organic'; he uses his attainments to discover new needs, and to assimilate new material. He lives from within outwards, his character is compact, coherent; he has *integrity.* The bad man, having no controlling unity, has no consistent line of action; his motives of conduct contradict one another; he follows this maxim in relation to this person, that in relation to another; character is *demoralized.*

The bad man is unstable and double-minded. He is not one person, but a group of conflicting wills. So far as he is really bad he becomes as many persons as he has desires. His conduct cannot be made universal. He always makes exceptions in favor of himself. He does not want moral relations abolished, but relaxed or deflected in his own case, while they still hold for other men.

This is the truth at the basis of Kant's contention regarding goodness as conduct whose maxim is capable of generalization. See also Bradley, Op. cit., pp. 261–271. And Alexander, Op. cit., pp. 309–312.

LXVIII.

Goodness in its Relation to the Struggle. 1. Two aspects of this we have already noted; one, that of conscientiousness, or habitual alertness and responsiveness of intelligence to the nature of obligation, both in general and as to the specific acts which are obligatory. The other is that goodness, in this relation, consists in *progressive* adjustment, involving aspiration as to future conduct, and correlative humility as to present achievements of character.

2. We may state what has already been suggested, that goodness as self-sacrifice or self-renunciation has also its place here. The moral attitude is one of renunciation, because, on account of the constantly growing wants and circumstances, the satisfactions which belong to the actually realized self must be given up for active goods. That the self-sacrifice takes largely the form of the surrender of private interests to the welfare of the whole, is explained by what has just been said regarding selfishness. Self-sacrifice is not in any way the moral end or the last word. Life is lost that it may be found. The smaller local life of the private self is given up in order that the richer and fuller life of the social or active self may be realized. But none the less the self-sacrifice at the time that it is made is genuine and real. While it is involved in the very nature of morality that moral conduct shall bring greater activity, larger life, the motive of the agent in self-sacrifice is not to give up the lesser satisfaction for the sake of getting a greater. It is only so far as he is already moral that he is convinced that the new duty will bring satis-

faction, and his conviction is not one of sense, but of faith. To the agent at the time of action, it is a real satisfaction which is given up for one that is only ideal, and given up because the ideal satisfaction is ethical, active — one congruent to duty, while the actual satisfaction is only pathological; that is, congruent to the actualized self—to the having, instead of the doing self.

3. Goodness is not remoteness from badness. In one sense, goodness is based upon badness; that is, good action is always based upon action good once, but bad if persisted in under changing circumstances. The moral struggle thus presents itself as the conflict between this "bad" and the good which would duly meet the existing situation. This good, of course, does not involve the annihilation of the previously attained good—the present bad—but its subordination; its use in the new function. This is the explanation of the apparently paradoxical statement that badness is the material of good action—a statement literally correct when badness is understood as it is here. Evil is simply that which goodness has to *overcome*—has to make an element of itself.

Badness, as just spoken of, is only potential—the end is bad as contrasted with the better. Badness may also, of course, be actual; the bad end may be chosen, and adopted into character. Even in this sense, goodness is not the absence of evil, or entire freedom from it. Badness even on this basis is the material of goodness; it is to be put under foot and made an element in good action. But how can actual evil be made a factor of right conduct? In this way; the good man learns from his own bad acts; he does not continue to repeat such acts, nor does he, while recognizing their badness, simply endeavor to do right without regard to the previous bad conduct. Perceiving the effect of his own wrong acts, the change produced in his own capacities, and his altered relations to other people, he acts so as to meet the situation which his own bad act has helped to create. Conduct is then right, although made what it is, to some degree, by previous wrong conduct.

In this connection, the introduction of Christianity made one of its largest ethical contributions. It showed how it was possible for a man to put his badness behind him and even make it an element in goodness. Teaching that the world of social relations was itself an ethical reality and a good (a redeemed world), it taught that the individual, by identifying himself with the spirit of this ethical world, might be freed from slavery to his past evil; that by recognizing and taking for his own the evil in the world, instead of engaging in an isolated struggle to become good by himself, he might make the evil a factor in his own right action.

Moreover, by placing morality in activity and not in some thing, or in conformity to an external law, Christianity changed the nature of the struggle. While the old struggle had been an effort to get away from evil to a good beyond, Christianity made the struggle itself a good. It, then, was no longer the effort to escape to some fixed, unchanging state; the constant onward movement was itself the goal. Virtue, as Hegel says, is the battle, the struggle, carried to its full.

4. *The conception of merit.* This is, essentially, the idea of social desert—the idea that an agent deserves well of others on account of his act or his character. An action evokes two kinds of judgments: first, that the act is right or virtuous, that it fulfills duty. This judgment may be passed by any one; as well by the agent as by any one else. It is simply the recognition of the moral character of the act. But a right act may also awaken a conviction of desert; that the act is one which furthers the needs of society, and thus is meritorious.

This is *not* a judgment which the agent can pass upon his own act. Virtue and duty are strictly coextensive; no act can be so virtuous, so right, as to go beyond meeting the demands of the situation. Everything is a duty which needs to be done in a given situation; the doing of what needs to be done is right or virtuous. While the agent may and must approve of right action in himself, he cannot claim desert or reward because of its virtuousness; he simply does what he should.

Others, however, may see that the act has been done in the face of great temptation; after a hard struggle; that it denotes some unusual qualification or executes some remarkable service. It is not only right, but obligatory, for others to take due notice of these qualities, of these deeds. Such notice is as requisite as it is to show gratitude for generosity, or forgiveness to a repentant man.

Two errors are to be avoided here; both arising from the identification of merit with virtue. One view holds that the virtue and merit consist in doing something over and above duty. There is a minimum of action which is obligatory; to perform this, since it is obligatory, is no virtue. Anything above this is virtuous. The other view reverses this and holds that since no man can do more than he ought, there is no such thing as merit. Great excellence or heroism in one man is no more meritorious than ordinary conduct in another; since the one man is naturally more gifted than the other. But while one act is no more right or virtuous than another, it may be more meritorious, because contributing more to moral welfare or progress. To depreciate the meritorious deed is a sign of a carping, a grudging or a mean spirit.

The respective relations of duty, virtue and merit have been variously discussed. Different views will be found in Sidgwick, Method of Ethics, Bk. III, ch. iv; Alexander, Moral Order and Progress, pp. 187–195 and 242–247; Stephen, Science of Ethics, pp. 293-303; Martineau, Types of Ethical Theory, pp. 78–81; Laurie, Ethica, pp. 145–148.

Chapter III. — REALIZED MORALITY OR THE VIRTUES.

LXIX.

Goodness as Found in Character. We have treated of the forming of moral ideals, and of the attempt to realize them against the counter attractions of sensible desire. We have now to treat these ideas as actual ends of conduct and thus reacting upon the agent. The good character, considered in relation to the moral *struggle*, is the one which chooses the right end, which endeavors to be better. The good character *in itself* is that made by this choice. It is good for the self to choose a due end in an effort caused by contrary allurements. But the very fact of the struggle witnesses that morality is not yet the natural and spontaneous manifestation of character. A *wholly* good man would feel such satisfaction in the contemplation of the ideal good that contrary desires would not affect him. He would take pleasure only in the right. Every accomplished moral deed tends to bring this about. Moral realization brings satisfaction. The satisfaction becomes one with the right act. Duty and desire grow into harmony. Interest and virtue tend toward unity.

This is the truth aimed at, but not attained, by the hedonistic school. In complete moral action, happiness and rightness know no divorce. And this is true, even though the act, in some of its aspects, involves pain. The act, so far as its quality of rightness is concerned, calls forth unalloyed satisfaction, however bound up with pain to self and to others in some respects. The error of hedonism is not in insisting that right action is pleasurable, but in its failure to supply content to the idea of happiness, in its failure to define what happiness is. In the failure to show those active relations of man to nature and to man involved in human satisfaction, it reduces happiness to the abstraction of agreeable sensation.

A virtue then, in the full sense, that is as the expression of virtuous character, and not of the struggle of character to be virtuous against the allurements of passive goods, is an *interest.* The system of virtues includes the various forms which interest assumes. Truthfulness, for example, is interest in the media of human exchange; generosity is interest in sharing any form of superior endowment with others less rich by nature or training, etc. It is distinguished from natural generosity, which may be mere impulse, by its being an interest in the activity or social relation itself, instead of in some accidental accompaniment of the relation.

Another way of getting at the nature of the virtues is to consider them as forms of freedom. Positive freedom is the good, it is realized activity, the full and unhindered performance of function. A virtue is any one aspect which the free performance of function may take. Meekness is one form of the adjustment of capacity to surroundings; honesty another; indignation another; scientific excellence another, and so on. In each of these virtues, the agent realizes his freedom: Freedom from subjection to caprice and blind appetite, freedom in the full play of activity.

LXX.

Two Kinds of Virtues. We may recognize two types of virtuous action. These are:

1. *The Special Virtues.* These arise from special capacities or special opportunities. The Greek sense of virtue was almost that of "excellence", some special fitness or power of an agent.

There is the virtue of a painter, of a scientific investigator, of a philanthropist, of a comedian, of a statesman, and so on. The special act may be manifested in view of some special occasion, some special demand of the environment — charity, thankfulness, patriotism, chastity, etc. Goodness, as the realization of the moral end, is a system, and the special virtues are the particular members of the system.

2. *Cardinal Virtues.* Besides these special members of a system, however, the whole system itself may present various aspects. That is to say, even in a special act the whole spirit of the man may be called out, and this expression of the whole character is a cardinal virtue. While the special virtues differ in content, as humility from bravery, earnestness from compassion, the cardinal virtues have the same content, showing only different sides of it. Conscientiousness, for example, is a cardinal virtue. It does not have to do with an act belonging to some particular capacity, or evoked by some special circumstance, but with the spirit of the whole self as manifested in the will to recognize duty—both its obligatoriness in general and the concrete forms which it takes. Truthfulness as a special virtue would be the desire to make word correspond to fact in some instance of speech. As a cardinal virtue, it is the constant will to clarify

and render true to their ideal all human relations—those of man to man, and man to nature.

LXXI.

The Cardinal Virtues. The cardinal virtues are marked by

1. *Wholeness.* This or that virtue, not calling the whole character into play, but only some special power, is partial. But a cardinal virtue is not *a* virtue, but the spirit in which all acts are performed. It lies in the attitude which the agent takes towards duty; his obedience to recognized forms, his readiness to respond to new duties, his enthusiasm in moving forward to new relations. It is a common remark that moral codes change from 'Do not' to 'Do', and from this to 'Be'. A Mosaic code may attempt to regulate the specific acts of life. Christianity says, 'Be ye perfect'. The effort to exhaust the various special right acts is futile. They are not the same for any two men, and they change constantly with the same man. The very words which denote virtues come less and less to mean specific acts, and more the spirit in which conduct occurs. Purity, for example, does not mean freedom from certain limited outward forms of defilement; but comes to signify rightness of natures as a whole, their freedom from all self-seeking or exclusive desire for private pleasure, etc. Thus purity of heart comes to mean perfect goodness.

2. *Disinterestedness.* Any act, to be virtuous, must of course be disinterested, but we may now connect this disinterestedness with the integral nature of moral action just spoken of. Immoral action never takes account of the whole nature of an end; it deflects the end to some ulterior purpose; it bends it to the private satisfaction of the agent; it takes a part of it by making exceptions in favor of self. Bad action is never 'objective'. It is 'abstract'; it takes into account only such portion of the act as satisfies some existing need of the private self. The immoral man shows his partial character again by being full of casuistries, devices by which he can get the act removed from its natural placing and considered in some other light:—this act, for example, *would* be dishonest, of course, if done under certain circumstances, but since I have certain praiseworthy feelings, certain remote intentions, it may now be considered otherwise. It is a large part of the badness of 'good' people that instead of taking the whole act just as it is, they endeavor to make the natural feelings in their own mind—feelings of charity, or benevolence—do substitute duty for the end aimed at; they excuse wrong acts on the ground that their 'intentions' were good, meaning by intentions the prevailing mood of their mind. It is in this sense that 'hell is paved with good intentions.'

Now it is against this deflection, perversion and mutilating of the act that disinterestedness takes its stand. Disinterested does not mean without interest, but without interest in anything except *the act itself*. The interest is not in the wonderful moods or sentiments with which we do the act; it is not in some ulterior end to be gained by it, or in some private advantage which it will bring, but in the act itself—in the real and concrete relations involved. There is a vague French saying that 'morality is the nature of things.' If this phrase has a meaning it is that moral conduct is not a manifestation of private feelings nor a search for some unattainable ideal, but observance and reproduction of actual relations. And this is the mark of a disinterested character.

CONCLUSION.

LXXII.

The Practical End of Morality. Virtues, then, are cardinal, and character is integral, just in the degree in which every want is a want of the whole man. So far as this occurs, the burden of the moral struggle is transformed into freedom of movement. There is no longer effort to bring the particular desire into conformity with a law, or a universal, outside itself. The fitting in of each special desire, as it arises, to the organism of character takes place without friction, as a natural re-adjustment. There is not constraint, but growth. On the other side, the attained character does not tend to petrify into a fixed possession which resists the response to needs that grow out of the enlarged environment. It is plastic to new wants and demands; it does not require to be wrenched and wracked into agreement with the required act, but moves into it, of itself. The law is not an external ideal, but the principle of the movement. There is the identity of freedom and law in the good.

This union of inclination and duty in act is the practical end. All the world's great reformers have set as their goal this ideal, which may be termed either the freeing of wants, or the humanizing of the moral law. It will help summarize our whole discussion, if we see how the theories of hedonism and of Kant have endeavored to express this same goal. Hedonism, indeed, has this identity for its fundamental principle. It holds strongly to the idea of moral law immanent in human wants themselves. But its error lies in taking this identity of desire and the good, as a direct or immediate unity, while, in reality, it exists only in and through activity; it is a unity which can be attained only as the result of a process. It mistakes an ideal which is realized only in action for bare fact which exists of itself.

Hedonism, as represented by Spencer, recognizes, it is true, that the unity of desire and duty is not an immediate or natural one; but only to fall into the error of holding that the separation is due to some external causes, and that when these are removed we shall have a fixed millenium. As against this doctrine, we must recognize that the difference between want and duty is always removed so far as conduct is moral; that it is not an ideal in the sense of something to be attained at some remote period, but an ideal in the sense of being the very meaning of moral activity whenever and wherever it occurs. The realizing of this ideal is not something to be sometime reached once for all, but progress is itself the ideal. Wants are ever growing larger, and thus freedom ever comes to have a wider scope (Sec. LXV).

Kant recognizes that the identity of duty and inclination is not a natural fact, but is the ideal. However, he understands by ideal something which ought to be, but is not. Morality is ever a struggle to get desire into unity with law, but a struggle doomed, by its very conditions, not to succeed. The law is the straight line of duty, which the asymptotic curve of desire may approximate, but never touch. An earthly taint of pleasure-seeking always clings to our wants, and makes of morality a striving which defeats itself.

The theory that morality lies in the realization of individuality recognizes that there is no direct, or natural, identity of desire and law, but also recognizes that their identification is not an impossible task. The problem is solved in the exercise of function, where the desires, however, are not unclothed, but clothed upon. Flowing in the channel of response to the demands of the moral environment, they unite, at once, social service and individual freedom.

LXXIII.

The Means of Moralization. This practical end of the unification of desire and duty, in the play of moral interests, is reached, therefore, so far as the desires are socialized. A want is socialized when it is not a want for its own isolated and fixed satisfaction, but reflects the needs of the environment. This implies, of course, that it is bound by countless ties to the whole body of desires and capacities. The eye, in seeing for itself, sees for the whole body, because it is not isolated but, through its connections, an organ of a system. In this same way, the satisfaction of a want for food, or for commercial activity, may necessitate a satisfaction of the whole social system.

But how shall this socialization of wants be secured? It is in answering this question that we are brought again to a point already discussed at length: the moral bearings of intelligence. It is intelligence that is the sole sure means of taking a want out of the isolation of merely impulsive action. It is the passing of the desire through the alembic of ideas that, in rationalizing and spiritualizing it, makes it an expression of the want of the whole man, and thus of social needs.

To know one's self was declared by Socrates, who first brought to conscious birth the spirit of the moral life, to be the very core of moral endeavor. This knowledge of self has taken, indeed, a more circuitous and a more painful path, than Socrates anticipated. Man has had, during two thousand years of science, to go around through nature to find himself, and as yet he has not wholly come back to himself—he oftentimes seems still lost in the wilderness of an outer world. But when man does get back to himself it will be as a victor laden with the spoils of subdued nature. Having secured, in theory and invention, his unity with nature, his knowledge of himself will rest on a wide and certain basis.

This is the final justification of the moral value of science and art. It is because through them wants are inter-connected, unified and socialized, that they are, when all is said and done, the pre-eminent moral means. And if we do not readily recognize them in this garb, it is because we have made of them such fixed things, that is, such abstractions, by placing them outside the movement of human life.

INDEX.